THE VIRTUE OF CIVILITY IN THE PRACTICE OF POLITICS

Philip D. Smith

University Press of America,® Inc.
Lanham · New York · Oxford

Copyright © 2002 by
University Press of America,® Inc.
4720 Boston Way
Lanham, Maryland 20706
UPA Acquisitions Department (301) 459-3366

12 Hid's Copse Rd.
Cumnor Hill, Oxford OX2 9JJ

Library of Congress Cataloging-in-Publication Data

Smith, Philip D.
The virtue of civility in the practice of politics / Philip D. Smith.
p.   cm
Includes bibliographical references and index.
1. Politics, Practical. 2. Civil society. 3. Courtesy. I. Title.

JF799 .S655 2002
172—dc21   2002020370 CIP

ISBN 0-7618-2329-8 (paperback : alk. ppr.)

This book is dedicated to my son James.

Contents

Preface

This is a book with possibly contradictory ambitions. I am a Christian, a philosopher, and a citizen, and I want to speak to audiences in all three directions.

My professional interests are in moral philosophy, so I want to pass muster in the guild; that is, I want other philosophers to test my ideas and arguments and find them worthy of discussion. As a Christian, I want other Christians to consider whether and how what I write here improves our understanding of our faith. As a citizen, I care about politics, and I hope other citizens will find what I write helpful as we seek together to create a just society.

Having more than one audience, I fear that philosophers and non-philosophers alike will be disappointed. Philosophers might complain that I seem to ignore important ideas or arguments in ethical theory, political philosophy, or philosophy of mind. Civility has connections with all these disciplines (and others), and I am aware that at many places I have not discussed them, but exploring these connections would make the book too long and restrict its audience to scholars. On the other hand, non-philosophers may think some parts of the book too technical as it is.

Of course, my fear is balanced by a hope: that philosophers will appreciate the arguments that are here rather than focus on those that are not, and that non-philosophers will tolerate some seemingly unnecessary detail while appreciating the book's main ideas.

For those main ideas are important. Several of these chapters have been presented to a variety of audiences, including philosophy conferences, Master of Business Administration classes, and the general public. Some of my readers or listeners have disagreed emphatically with my proposals, but few have thought that the topic is unimportant. Civility is something many people seem to want, even if we disagree about what it is.

In moral philosophy I am what is known as a "virtue theorist." I think that much (not all) of our moral life is better understood in terms of virtues--character traits--than in terms of actions or rules for acting. In simplest terms, the fundamental idea of this book, one which occured to me some years ago, is that civility is a virtue related to the political opponent. I have been exploring some of the implications of that idea since then, and this book is the result.

In this book I offer definitions of several words: civility, politics, opponent, coercion, pacifism, etc. The conclusions I reach, such as they are, often depend on the meanings of these words as I define them. Readers may suspect that this is a pretty poor way to do philosophy; if one defines terms as one likes, one can push the discussion wherever he wants. But that is not my intention. Rather, I want to reduce obscurity. Moral philosophy (like many other disciplines) is often confused by muddled ideas. By giving definitions of important terms, I hope the reader will be clear about what I am saying, even if she disagrees with it.

I hold to romantic goals in moral philosophy. I hope to say something both true and useful about my topic. "Useful" here would mean saying something which actually helps people develop the virtue of civility. It may be hoped that even if what I say isn't true--in the sense my main ideas are fundamentally flawed--the book may still be useful, for readers who discover such flaws will presumably be more able to understand and pursue civility better by avoiding them.

I need to thank several people for their help. Paul Anderson, Richard Engnell, Mark Hall, Mark McLeod, and Ron Mock, colleagues at George Fox University, have read parts or the whole of the manuscript and corrected many errors. I had the delight of discussing chapter eight with Robert Adams, Robert Roberts, and Robert Wennberg at a Society of Christian Philosophers conference at Westmont College in April 2001. Bennet Smith, a student at George Fox, also contributed helpful feedback. All of these readers offered advice which I decided not to follow, so it's clear that the remaining defects of the book are due to my own stubbornness rather than their advice.

I thank the faculty development committee of George Fox University, which supported the writing of several chapters with summer research grants.

I thank my wife, Karen, and my son, Timothy, for their encouragement of my work. A particular thank you goes to my younger son, James, who in the last few years has taught me more about civility in the real world than anyone. To James, and our struggles together, this book is dedicated.

Chapter One:

Controversies and Conduct

Consider controversies and the ways we conduct them. Here are some recent examples.

1. Corporate Policy. The annual shareholder meeting of a large, U.S. based apparel manufacturer draws near. On the agenda of the meeting is a shareholder proposal that the company adopt a policy of paying a "living wage" to the workers, usually in third world countries, who make the company's products. The proposal requires that the company make sure this policy applies to workers for subcontractors as well—no hiding behind some smaller local company whose whole business is supplying goods to the parent company.

Some people, including the top executives of the company, argue that markets set wages and prices; if the company tries to ignore such realities, it will inevitably fail. They vigorously oppose the proposal. The supporters of the living wage proposal deny that their proposal threatens profitability (they point out that doubling or even tripling the wages of the third world apparel workers would increase final costs of the product only marginally), and they argue that corporations have responsibilities to workers that go beyond market wages.

How might the two sides in this debate conduct themselves? It would be easy enough to make this illustration specific and write about how people have actually conducted themselves; several U.S. based corporations have found themselves in this controversy. But I have told a generic story in order to avoid actual cases and ask how *might* the sides to the controversy conduct the debate—that is, what are the *possible* ways people handle such situations?

Does the first side—led by the company's officers—insist that only stockholders have a voice in the debate? Should that voice be strictly apportioned to the number of their shares? Let's suppose there are protesters outside the building where the stockholders' meeting takes place; should protesters have a voice in company policy? Should third-world workers—workers for a subcontractor, perhaps—have a voice in company policy? Would it make a difference if those workers had a union? Should consumers, expressing themselves through a boycott or by buying products wearing a "SAFE" label[1], have a voice in this debate?

Notice that these questions focus on *who should be involved* in a controversy. Let's keep that question in mind for a while and look at another example.

2. Church Policy. The regional governing structure of a protestant denomination is considering whether to ordain lesbians or gay men to the ministry. (Once again the example is generic; several denominations have faced this question. The question, with slight changes, has also come up in Roman Catholic and Jewish faith communities.) One side argues that the church ought to ordain gays, because God loves and accepts gays and because the candidate ministers have demonstrated their gifts for ministry—the church needs such leadership! In opposition, others say that God does indeed love gays, but God rejects homosexual behavior, so the candidate ministers are contradicting Christian doctrine by their behavior, and therefore they should not be ordained. To ordain them would be plain disobedience to God!

How do the opponents in this dispute conduct the dispute? Does the first side insist that it is impossible to accept a gay person without accepting his sexual orientation? Do they notice, as their opponents will, that this insistence implies that their opponents don't really love gays? Do they angrily reject the other side's analogy: that one can love and accept an alcoholic without accepting alcoholism?

Does the second side insist that it is impossible to read scripture faithfully and still think that God accepts homosexual behavior? Do they notice, as their opponents will, how this insistence implies that their opponents don't obey scripture? Do they label the candidate gay ministers as perverts or deviants? Do they angrily reject the other side's analogy: that discrimination against gays is just like discrimination on the basis of race?

Notice that these questions focus on analogies, metaphors and reasoning processes. Often a controversy is not just about what we should do, it's also about how we should think about the controversy. What are the right categories or tools for this dispute? We might be tempted to think we ought always to discuss issues in objective, morally neutral terms in order to avoid bias, but that can't be right. Sometimes the only true word is a "judgmental" word.[2] Just as often, though, persons in controversies say what they think is true only to have "truth" alienate others and close the door to creative solutions. So how should we think about controversies? Again, let's hold this question for later and look at another example.

3. Public Policy.   Under the U. S. Constitution, do state governments have the authority to regulate or prohibit very late term abortions? If the U. S. Supreme Court holds that states have this authority, should they exercise it?

Some people say that these abortions, which they call partial birth abortions, are nothing short of murder, since at thirty or thirty-two weeks of fetal development, the fetuses in these cases very closely resemble children who have already been born. In opposition, other people claim that such abortions are rare, and they are needed because of the unusual circumstances accompanying some pregnancies. This side resists any law that would chip away at the fundamental right of self-determination for women, which they say begins with the ability to choose whether to bear children.

How do the debaters conduct this controversy? In recent decades we have become familiar with the labels and slogans of abortion: pro-life vs. pro-choice, the right to choose vs. the right to life, and on and on. It often seems that the slogans offered by the contestants are designed to inspire commitment in their base constituency rather than solve a problem. Both sides readily supply labels which rhetorically box-in and delegitimize their opponents. The very words of the debate seem to keep moderates out of the discussion.

So how should we talk about abortion? Is a baby a "baby" before it is born? Does a doctor who performs a late term abortion "kill" the fetus? If she does, does that make her a killer? If a man is "anti-choice," is he then anti-woman?

Notice here that we are asking about words and labels—for actions, attitudes, and persons. What words should we use in controversies?

How should we talk about issues? How should we talk about people on the other side?

Let's review. There are at least three clusters of issues that relate to the way people conduct controversies; these clusters correspond to the questions, "Who should be involved in the controversy?" "How should we think about the controversy?" and "What words should we use to describe the controversy and the people involved in it?"

By now, the reader has noticed that my primary interest is in the way we should conduct controversies, not solutions or answers to the examples I have mentioned. This doesn't mean I am uninterested in business ethics, moral theology, or political philosophy or in the particular examples I've used to illustrate them. On the contrary, it is because we desire to find the truth about such matters that I suggest we ought to pay attention to *how* we conduct controversies. Three important ideas, which will resurface repeatedly in this book, are bound up in the notion of the conduct of controversies.

First, *process*: we should think of controversies as processes. Controversies manifest themselves in lots of ways—as debates, discussions, fights, wars, smoldering resentments, elections, protest marches, boycotts, etc.—but they are never static. Controversies have histories: beginnings, middles, and ends. Controversies move, and we should ask where they are going.

Second, *truth*: we should believe that controversies can, and therefore should, aim at discovering truth.[3] Some people do not think about controversies this way. They see controversies as contests, zero-sum games, win-lose battles. This book will suggest that, citing Mohandas Gandhi and some current literature in business management, controversies do not have to produce losers. Instead controversies can produce truth.

To anticipate: these first two points suggest guidelines for the first two question-clusters, "Who should be involved in the controversy?" and "How should we think about the controversy?" If a controversy is a process aimed at discovering truth, then the people who can best help discover the truth should be involved. I will contend that those people are usually our political opponents. Again, if a controversy is a process aimed at discovering truth, the metaphors and analogies we use to think about the controversy should be those that help us find truth. I won't try to develop these ideas now; we will return to them in later chapters.

Third, *civility*: as the title makes clear, this is the main emphasis of the book. My thesis is this: there is a virtue—civility—that we ought to seek, which is the appropriate virtue for controversies, because it focuses on the political opponent. Since "political" (in a sense I will make clear later) controversies occupy a large place in our lives, this virtue of civility should have a correspondingly high place in our moral vocabulary.

To advance this thesis, I will take some space in the next chapter, "A Definition of Civility," to explain what I mean by civilit, a word that has been used variously by many authors, especially recently, and to defend civility as I define it against several misunderstandings of it. In chapter three, "The Virtue of Civility in the Practice of Politics," I will explore the nature of civility further, making use of work of Alasdair MacIntyre, and applying civility to politics in the world of business.

In chapter four, "Robert Audi's Rules of Christian Citizenship," I begin to examine the place of civility in public politics. Although he doesn't use the language of virtues or "civility," I believe Robert Audi's writing on Christian citizenship raises sharp questions about civility. I try to point out things we can learn from Audi, but I also criticize his ideas as giving an unsatisfactory account of civility because it rests on modern (i.e. Enlightenment) assumptions about citizenship. Chapter five, "Civil Speech, the Right, and the Good," goes deeper into political philosophy, examining the work of Mark Kingwell and others who have made the interesting suggestion that civility—understood as a kind of self-imposed constraint on speech—could be very important to, perhaps even definitive of, justice in a liberal state. I argue that Kingwell and company are right to emphasize the importance of civil speech, right to think that justice is enmeshed with civility, but wrong to think civility can be maintained unless it is grounded in some substantive conception of the good life.

Having criticized Audi and Kingwell (and by implication, many other philosophers) for mistakenly trying to ground civility in Enlightenment philosophy, in chapter six, "A Basis for Civility," I discuss the rise of civility, a history in which both religious arguments and Enlightenment philosophy play roles. Do I, then, contradict myself? I will explain how the contradiction is only apparent, and I will suggest a pre-modern basis for civility that satisfactorily grounds our pursuit of this virtue.

Chapter seven, "Civility and a Civil Process," does not say much about the virtue of civility as such, but tries to anticipate practical questions readers may have about a truth seeking process. I have little original to say on the topic, so the chapter mostly points the reader to good sources.

Perhaps the most difficult aspect of civility, at least as I present it in this book, has to do with coercion. In chapter eight, "Civility and Coercion," I begin with a quote from Richard Mouw and explore in some detail the relationship between the virtue of civility and possible justifications for coercion. In an addendum to that chapter I ask whether civility pushes one toward pacifism. Chapter nine, "What Next?" briefly reviews the book's main ideas and suggests aspects of civility that ought to be explored more thoroughly.

An Initial Objection

Some readers[4] will object that study of civility—no matter how it is defined—can never be more than a subordinate topic in moral philosophy. As John Rawls said, *justice* is the first virtue of social institutions.[5] An uncivil, but just, society would surely be a better place than an unjust, but civil society. Shouldn't we be clear with ourselves, these objectors will say, that our study of civility is a matter of filling in the small corners of political morality?

Take, for example, the debate over slavery in the nineteenth century in the United States. The objector will point out that on any plausible definition of civility, we can easily find examples of incivility on both sides of that debate. If we peruse histories of the antebellum period, there will be examples of pro-slavery people conducting the controversy abominably. They ridiculed the abolitionists, they mistrusted the intentions of moderates, they manipulated political procedures, and they used placid euphemisms to talk about gross injustice and cruelty. But for every example of pro-slavery incivility, we can find another (perhaps worse) example of incivility by the abolitionist movement. The abolitionists also heaped scorn on moderates, caricatured their opponents as enemies of humanity, and quite deliberately described themselves as prophets of a higher morality, as the mouthpieces of God.

How could we judge one side as more uncivil than the other? The objector will press his case: what difference would it make if we could? For sake of argument, the objector says, let's accept two stereotypes, which lived long in the South: the abolitionist as rude, self-righteous, and small-minded and the plantation owner as civil, genteel, and sophisticated. In other words, picture the abolitionist as uncivil as you like and the pro-slavery person as civil as possible. Still, the objector says, the only important fact about the debate is that the abolitionists were right and the pro-slavery people were wrong. No matter how civil or genteel they were, the pro-slavery people were defending a moral outrage. Why? Because slavery is fundamentally unjust, and justice is the most important virtue of a good society. Reflecting on the slavery debate and on the Congressional "gag rule" of the 1830s and 1840s[6], James Schmidt concludes, "Civility may well be a virtue. But it is probably not a virtue that will be of much help in deciding the political questions that ultimately matter."[7]

So goes the objection. How can I defend my project against such an argument? Do I want to say that civility, however I define it, is more important than justice?

As a preliminary response, let's suppose we accepted Rawls' dictum that justice is the first virtue of social institutions. That does not make civility unimportant, only less important than justice. Perhaps there are many other virtues of civil society.[8] (In the next chapter I will suggest that there are, and that writers like Stephen Carter have made discussion of civility unnecessarily complicated by lumping a variety of virtues together under the label of civility.) Civility could turn out to be high on the list and well worth our study, even if justice always trumps civility.

But it is not clear that justice does trump civility. To see why, let's return to case of slavery and note that there are contemporary controversies in which this example is cited explicitly. Anti-abortion activists, to take one group, sometimes portray themselves as inheriting the mantle of abolition. Just as the abolitionists had grasped the crucial truth about slavery (Slaves are human beings with human rights; human rights include life and liberty; so . . .), the pro-lifers are convinced they see clearly the crucial truth about abortion (Fetuses are human beings with human rights; human rights include life and liberty; so . . .). These pro-lifers will point out that their nineteenth century forefathers (and foremothers—the abolition movement was sprinkled with women leaders, who can be quoted, conveniently enough, as strongly opposing abortion as well as slavery!) were often accused of being uncivil. Remember a familiar picture of an abolitionist: self-righteous, loud, rude, insistent, morally imperialistic, maybe even messianic—John Brown or William Lloyd Garrison. If this caricature isn't fair to many abolitionists of the actual past, it is nevertheless the way many Southerners thought of abolitionists, and there were enough John Brown types to give it substance. The pro-lifers conclude that it doesn't matter if *they* are rude, loud, self-righteous, etc. Their lack of civility is far less important than their accurate judgment on a matter of justice. Just as the nineteenth century abolitionists were right about slavery, the twenty-first century abolitionists are right about abortion. Justice trumps civility.

Consider that "abortion abolitionists" are only one illustration of this kind of argument. Similar justifications can be, and are, offered by "nuclear weapons abolitionists,"[9] World Trade Organization protesters, Marxist-Leninists, and many others. The argument fits a pattern, which I will discuss as the "logic of intolerance" in chapter six. In each case, the argument concludes by agreeing with the objector that justice trumps civility.

How do pro-choice people respond to this move of the pro-lifers, when the pro-lifers wrap themselves in the mantle of abolition? Obviously, they think it is unfair, because it is inaccurate. Slavery really is fundamentally unjust, but abortion isn't. In fact, abortion rights activists say, it is their side which truly recognizes the full humanity denied by others—the full humanity of women, which is denied by a paternalistic mind set that would take away a woman's control over her own life.

The slavery analogy becomes very hard to apply when it comes to abortion. Who are the rightful heirs of the abolitionist mantle?

I suggest that the "justice trumps civility" rule is just as hard to apply as the slavery analogy. Said in another way, it is too easy to apply. All one has to do is say, "My side is right on an important matter, a matter of basic justice. In defense or pursuit of justice, we will try to be civil, but we will not allow civility to stand in the way of justice." It seems that something is going wrong if the priority of justice over civility gives comfort to so many different groups on opposing sides of many controversies. Can we say where the mistake is?

The mistake in the objection (summed up as "justice trumps civility") is the assumption that justice can be known without civility. In this book I will suggest that civility, rightly understood, is deeply enmeshed in justice. If we engage in a controversy without civility, we greatly weaken our chances of finding justice in that debate. Human beings are neither omniscient nor morally perfect, and our judgments are limited by our lack of knowledge and our moral failings. Thus, we are always in pursuit of justice, both in our understanding of it and our practice of it. Of course, our understanding of justice interweaves with our practice of justice. All virtues have this double aspect; learning them involves intellectual gain mixed with practice.

The pursuit of justice involves us with other people, for two reasons. First, because justice is a social virtue, we practice it in our relationships with others. Second, we partially overcome our intellectual weaknesses when we work together. The project of understanding justice, even theoretically, is a task for philosophical discussion, not only individual philosophical reflection.[10]

Since we pursue justice with others, civility is crucial to that pursuit. Civility is the virtue which more than any other contributes to the success of groups working together, because civility invites the contribution of resources, resources supplied by the political opponent, which we are most in danger of missing. These claims cannot be defended without offering a definition of civility, the task of the next chapter. But if I am right about the role of civility in discovering and practicing justice, then it is wrong, or at least misleading, to say that justice trumps civility.

Return one last time to the slavery debate. Slavery was and is a great moral wrong, and justice demands the abolition of slavery. So the abolitionists were right. But did the abolitionists know they were right?

Since Plato, philosophers have carefully distinguished being right from knowing one is right. Suppose someone took his struggling business's cash box to Vegas, believing that his good luck would enable him to escape a tight spot. And he was right; his gambling winnings saved the company! We can imagine that he had strong confidence that he would win, but we still judge that he did not know he would win. Knowledge requires something more than true belief. I am not going to launch into a discussion of epistemology at this point; we do not need to know exactly what this "something more" is in order to proceed.[11] Whatever the "something more" is that we need to really know something, it's clear that the gambler doesn't have it. Confidence alone, a psychological state, doesn't change belief into knowledge, even if one turns out to be right. Now, did the abolitionists have this "something more"? We hesitate to say yes, because we remember that the slavery defenders resembled the abolitionists in so many ways. The abolitionists were sure of their convictions, but so were slave owners. The abolitionists defended their views by appealing to scripture, so did the slave owners. The abolitionists risked life, limb, and social prestige to eliminate slavery; slave owners matched their efforts to protect slavery. And so on.

Let's come at the question from a different angle. Suppose we were abolitionists living in the 1850s. We would have strong feelings, moral intuitions, against slavery. But questions might rise in our mind: do we know that slavery is wrong? How could we know that slavery is wrong? These questions bother us all the more when we consider how many well-educated, thoughtful, humane people defended slavery.

There is a way to test moral intuitions, in order to move them toward knowledge, or to change them, if it turns out they are wrong. We can seek moral knowledge, confirming or disconfirming our feelings, by means of controversies, if we conduct our controversies properly. I will describe a truth seeking process in chapter seven.

The opponent in a controversy offers an invaluable resource in the search for truth. Because the opponent believes something different than we do, he is highly motivated to show us the weaknesses in our reasoning and point out evidence we may have ignored. If we can conduct our controversy in such a way that we can genuinely hear the opponent's objections, we greatly increase our chances of subjecting our moral intuitions to the strongest criticism. Only moral intuitions that emerge from the fire of this kind of testing can be candidates for moral knowledge.

Imagine, then, that as nineteenth century abolitionists we engaged the pro-slavery people (who, after all, were our fellow citizens) in a civil controversy. We welcomed their arguments as the best challenges to our own views. We persisted with them in an energetic and emotionally difficult debate. In the end, we came to agree that slavery is wrong (and in the process we came to know that slavery is wrong[12]), and found a way to bring slavery to an end in America.

Perhaps this scenario will strike some people as hopelessly naive. Slavery was entrenched in the South, they will say, and only the Civil War could have brought its end.

Is that true?

Let's not assume that what did happen had to happen. Slavery did end in America by means of the Civil War. In the half century after the Civil War, it did become clear to almost all Americans that slavery is morally wrong. But that things did go that way does not show that things had to go that way. Great Britain, during the same period when the U.S. was moving toward the Civil War, eliminated slavery without war. Perhaps, if the abolitionists had pursued their cause differently, the end of slavery in the U.S. could have come without the horrendous scars of the Civil War.

Now, some will say that peculiarities of American slavery and the American political situation precluded any other outcome rather than war. Maybe they are right; perhaps in the case of the slavery controversy the way things did happen was the way things had to happen. But consider this. Ought we to think that *our* controversies *now* are like that? Should we think that the conflict between the WTO and the protesters, between pro-life and pro-choice—in general, between "us" and "them"—is ultimately a matter of force? Is warfare how we hope to educate ourselves (and, of course, "them") about right and wrong?

No. We must learn to conduct our controversies as truth seeking processes. To succeed, we must learn to be civil. I turn next to a definition of civility.

Notes

[1] See Benjamin Barber, *A Place for Us* (New York: Hill and Wang, 1998), pp. 102-03 for a description of efforts to identify and mark apparel products manufactured under "safe" —child labor safe, fair wage safe, workplace safe, and environmentally safe—conditions.

[2] Edwin J. Delattre recounts an example in which an educational bias review committee objected to the description of Stalin as "ruthless," because "that might offend the emotional sensibilities of socialist students." Stalin really was ruthless, and Delattre argues that it is a disservice to students to imply otherwise. See "Civility and the Limits to the Tolerable" in *Civility*, ed. Leroy S. Rouner (Notre Dame, Indiana: University of Notre Dame Press, 2000), p. 152.

[3] This is a place—there will be many in this book—where responding to philosophical controversies could easily derail my essay. For example, Richard Rorty has suggested that "truth" is an unhelpful word in our politico-ethical tradition, since it implies an impossible picture of our noetic capacities ("the mind as mirror of the world") and it invariably is used to justify power and coercion. Not many philosophers have been persuaded by Rorty, and I certainly am not. But it would distract terribly from my project to discuss Rorty's "ironism" with the attention it deserves here.

[4] That is, if they are readers at all—people who strongly object in this way may have abandoned the book already!

[5] John Rawls, *A Theory of Justice* (Cambridge, Massachusetts: Harvard University Press, 1971), p. 3.

[6] In order to keep the slavery debate from stopping work on other issues, Congress adopted a rule that forbade the discussion of slavery during many of its sessions.

---

[7] James Schmidt, "Is Civility a Virtue?" in *Civility*, Ed. Leroy S. Rouner (Notre Dame, Indiana: University of Notre Dame Press, 2000), p. 37.

[8] As Rawls recognized. See *A Theory of Justice*, p. 9.

[9] Notice how the very word, abolition, puts a rhetorical cast on a movement. In a contrary way, "prohibition" can be used to make one's opponents' proposals seem impractical.

[10] What I am doing right now, writing a chapter of a book of moral philosophy, probably looks more like individual philosophical reflection than a discussion. But a book of philosophy should be considered a contribution to ongoing discussion rather than the last word of polished wisdom. I am certainly grateful for the conversations with other philosophers which this project has occasioned.

[11] For a helpful survey and pointed criticism of contemporary theory of knowledge, see Alvin Plantinga, *Warrant: the Current Debate* (New York: Oxford University Press, 1993).

[12] I am not claiming that agreement—contractual, consensual, or of any sort—is the defining mark of moral knowledge. I am only saying that often in the process of gaining agreement we find that we have gained moral knowledge. Remember, here I am not offering any detailed account of warrant, whether of moral knowledge or of knowledge in general. For a challenging recent account of warrant, see Alvin Plantinga, *Warrant and Proper Function* (New York: Oxford University Press, 1993).

Chapter Two:

A Definition of Civility

In the 1990s, civility became something of a hot topic. Distressed by dirty tricks in political campaigns, road rage on freeways, rude clerks in stores, intemperate voices on talk radio shows, and other examples of bad behavior, thoughtful people called for a return to virtue, and they called the virtue civility. A quick literature survey would find hundreds of editorials, dozens of scholarly articles, and several books that address civility in some way.[1]

It becomes clear when sampling what people have said about civility that they aren't all talking about the same thing. James Schmidt observed about the notion of civility that "it is something which a good many people are inclined to promote, even though they may not be entirely sure what it is that they are promoting."[2] To illustrate the vagueness of "civility," Schmidt points to the "Rules of Civility and Decent Behavior in Company and in Conversation" which George Washington copied as a manual of self-direction. Some of Washington's rules enjoin what we would consider moral precepts: to show respect to others and keep conscience alive. Others, though, tell the civil person how to dress, how to sit at dinner, what not to do when walking down the street, which superiors one ought to honor by removing one's hat, how to fold napkins, how to avoid spitting in someone's face, and many other things which to us seem to be matters of etiquette, and an archaic etiquette at that.[3] (This is not to imply that etiquette is unimportant; I will say more about it later.)

We might begin by thinking that civility is a virtue proper to "civil society," but it turns out that "civil society" is subject to as many interpretations as "civility."[4] For Aristotle, *koinonia politike* denoted the political community as opposed to the household (*oikos*). Florentine humanist Leonardo Bruni translated Aristotle's phrase as *societas civilis*, and "civil society" entered the Western political lexicon. But it did not always retain its meaning as something differentiated from the household.

For Augustine, the city of God was opposed to the city of man, so some of our tradition (i.e. Hobbes or Hegel) distinguishes civil society from ecclesiastical society. For social contract theorists, civilized life is opposed to the state of nature, so civil society is the non-natural realm. For Locke, civil society is not civil government (a society remains the same society even if the people exercise their right to change governments). Hegel and Tocqueville push this idea further; for them civil society is not government or church or (for Hegel) family. Hegel thought that competition in the market would educate individuals, transforming self-concerned *bourgeois* into true citizens, *citoyen*. For some, civil society is not military society. Often in our history, civil society has been opposed to "barbarian" society, and an association between "civility" and proper manners resulted.

A contemporary writer, Benjamin Barber, contrasts civil society with government and market (in stark contrast to Hegel).[5] With some hesitation, Barber includes churches as civil institutions, and Stephen Carter thinks religion is necessary to a healthy civil society[6] —both authors contrasting sharply with Hegel and others.

So: civil society is political (Aristotle), but not political (Locke, Barber). It does not refer to the family (Aristotle, Hegel), but it applies to the family (Carrie Doehring[7]). It is the market realm (Hegel), but it is not the market realm (Barber). It includes religious institutions (Barber, Carter), but it is not ecclesiastical (Hegel, Augustine).

I suggest that trying to understand civility by tying it to "civil society" is a dead end. Instead, we should think of civility as a virtue in Aristotelian terms, that is, as a functional characteristic, something the possession of which helps one achieve success in some activity or another. In the next chapter, following the work of Alasdair MacIntyre, I will describe the conceptual apparatus of practices, institutions and virtues that underlies a functional understanding of virtues. Here, my immediate task is to offer a definition of civility (and definitions of politics and political opponent, in terms of which civility is to be understood) and to defend civility against some possible misunderstandings.

Civility and Politics

I begin by offering the following definition: *Civility is a properly grounded character trait which moves an individual to treat political opponents well and/or to feel certain emotions toward political opponents, emotions which move an individual to treat political opponents well.*

Thus defined, civility disposes one to certain behaviors and/or certain emotions. Stephen Carter suggests "respect," "awe," and "gratitude" as the emotions a civil person is disposed to have in the presence of other people.[8] Perhaps "love" or other emotions should be included. The emotions the civil person is disposed to feel toward political opponents reinforce the disposition to act in a certain way, that is, to treat political opponents well.

Let us use here a broad understanding of politics and political opponent. The second definition: *Politics is the art or science of making decisions for groups of people.* Notice that with this definition we may speak of office politics, church politics, university politics, electoral politics, etc., which accords with much ordinary usage, but which differs from the language of many political philosophers, who reserve "politics" for governmental affairs. Benjamin Barber, for example, defines "civil society" as that "space" between government and market organizations.[9] He sees significant differences between our roles and responsibilities in government on one side, in business on another, and "civil society" on a third. Differences there are, but the commonalities are fundamental; in each space individuals must work together to decide their course, often in the context of large institutions. They agree and disagree; they make enemies and alliances; they compromise, conquer, or create third options; and they struggle, in all this, to do the right thing and be good people. The broad definition of politics I am offering helps us see the moral connectedness of life.[10]

Let us delete any negative connotation from this understanding of politics. Groups have to make decisions; politics aims at good decisions. The third definition follows from the second: *Political opponents are people who have conflicts over group decision proposals*, whether those decisions are about things the group is to believe or do. Again, let's use political opponent as a neutral term; sometimes political opponents become enemies and spend their energy trying to defeat each other, but sometimes political opponents allow their differences to push them toward creativity and better decisions. To be a political opponent and to have political opponents are not bad things.

Let's go back to "civility." Much of the work of my definition of civility is done by the word, "well." Civil people are moved to treat political opponents well and/or to have emotions that move them to treat political opponents well. Negatively, this means we (if we are civil) are disposed to not impugn opponents' motives, slander them, lie to them, ignore them, or the like. Positively, we are disposed to debate honestly with them, keep any agreements we make with them, treat them with dignity, and so on. Fortunately, the notion of treating someone well is widely understandable, even without an exhaustive list of specific prohibitions or prescriptions.

The remainder of this chapter will try to fill out some of the implications of this definition of civility by guarding it against four possible misunderstandings.

Civility Clarified

1. Civility is not politeness. People often confuse civility with politeness, and understandably so, as they are related concepts. Like civility, politeness is a virtue, and like civility it aims at treating people well (at least usually). We who study civility may well gain insight into our topic by hearing what the purveyors of politeness have to say about theirs.[11]   But the two virtues apply to different practices with different social backgrounds.[12]

Politeness focuses closely on the rules of etiquette. Polite people are motivated to obey etiquette rules, which describe behavior appropriate to certain social situations.[13]   Rules of etiquette are highly dependent on concrete social environments, which vary over time and geography. The rules of proper behavior at the court of Elizabeth II are different from those of the court of Elizabeth I, and both sets of rules differ from those that applied to Cleopatra's court. Obviously, etiquette rules may exist for many other social circumstances; these three courts merely illustrate the point. Perhaps we may broaden the notion of "court" to cover any specifiable social circumstance in which particular mores are recognized as proper, correct or permissible. A polite person would be motivated to learn and obey the rules of proper behavior in whatever setting or "court" she found herself. Politeness as a virtue is less tied to specific circumstances than are the rules of etiquette.

In a sense, civility is narrower than politeness. The rules of etiquette address, depending on particular social situations, a bewildering variety of human behaviors—the proper way to eat, speak, conduct duels, defecate, make love, read poetry, treat servants, behave in movie theatres, and so on—and the polite person is motivated to keep them. Civility, as I am proposing to understand it, focuses on politics—group decision-making—and on political opponents. Many of the situations addressed by rules of etiquette are irrelevant to politics.

Etiquette experts would tell us that polite persons do not learn and obey rules of etiquette merely for the sake of the rules. Polite people care about other people; they have enough good sense to learn and use the conventional ways of expressing care for others.[14]   In this regard, civility is like politeness, in that both virtues are rooted in a recognition of the worth of other people. But politeness is tied to the rules of etiquette in a way that civility is not. This brings me to the second misunderstanding of civility.

2. Civility is not a tool for repression. A philosopher friend once asked me if civility were not a "white guy virtue." That is, civility might be something socially advantaged people (whites, males) could afford, but might stand in the way of justice for the powerless. She worried that a concern for civility—misunderstood perhaps as polite speech in political processes—could be used to repress people. It almost always happens that politically disadvantaged groups have less training in the rules of etiquette than the wealthy or the powerful. If the powerful people at "court" require that all political speech be polite speech, many of the poor or powerless will be politically speechless. The rules of etiquette become a barrier that keeps people out of political discussion. And this has actually happened at many times in many courts. Etiquette experts might protest that this abuse doesn't represent true politeness—after all, it isn't polite to use the rules of etiquette to repress others—but we will not stop here to explore defenses of politeness.

Civility, as I understand it, does not focus on the rules of etiquette. It focuses on the political opponent, and consists in a disposition to treat the political opponent well and/or to feel emotions that dispose one to treat political opponents well. Often, a civil person may find herself obeying the rules of etiquette, perhaps without knowing them, but she may also break etiquette rules precisely because she is civil. An illustration from history may help.

In seventeenth century England, Quakers were often arrested. They were eager to defend themselves in court, since they saw this as an opportunity to "publish truth." But their attempts at defending themselves often foundered on the shoals of etiquette. Etiquette at that time directed persons (if they were men) to show honor to judges by removing hats in court[15] and addressing judges in the formal "you," rather than the familiar "thee" or "thou." Quakers objected to these rules of honor, and they regularly addressed judges as "thee" or "thou" or (even better) "friend" so-and-so. (Current etiquette directs that we stand when judges enter court. Modern Quakers don't seem to object to this; one might wonder if we are less concerned with equality or just less prickly.) Clearly, these Quakers were impolite, but it is not at all clear that they were uncivil. They claimed that they were motivated by concern for the judges when they refused them hat honor or addressed them as "friend." If we take their claims at face value, their impolite actions were civil actions, springing from emotions of regard and care for their political opponents.

The tactics of Mohandas Gandhi and Martin Luther King, Jr. also illustrate the distinction between civility and politeness. A protest march almost surely violates the rules of etiquette. By definition, illegal demonstrations violate the rules of political speech as defined by the powers that be. But King and Gandhi repeatedly emphasized the idea that their tactics were aimed at the opponents' good as well as the good of their own people. Both leaders urged members of their movements to be genuinely disposed to treat opponents well, especially when their actions of protest stirred the opponents to violence.

These examples should remind us that civility is a virtue of politically active people; in no way does it require passivity. On the contrary: one must be involved in the political process—group decision making—in order to have political opponents in relation to which one can be civil. Debate between political opponents can be vigorous, emphatic, and principled and still be marked by emotions of respect, care, and even awe for the political opponent.

3. A third misunderstanding of civility is that it consists in rules and rule keeping. I've already proposed that civility does not focus on the rules of etiquette; now I am saying it doesn't focus on rules at all.

The revival of virtue theory in the late twentieth century has become a staple item of introductory ethics classes. All our textbooks have at least a chapter on virtue theory, and whatever a philosopher's own theoretical leaning, he will include a lecture or two on virtue in ethics courses. Through familiarity, we run a risk of trivializing something important.

There is a fundamental shift in moral philosophy when we move our focus from action to character. This shift does not happen easily; for at least some of us it is a struggle. For whatever cause, perhaps our early childhood training or something else, we find it natural to think about ethics in terms of rules: lists of prohibitions and prescriptions. I am not here speaking of *philosophical* reasons for including rules and rule-keeping as topics in ethical theory; I readily grant there may be good arguments along those lines. I am speaking of a *psychological* predisposition to assume that ethics is about rules. Maybe this isn't a problem for others; I know it is for me. So I have to be careful and deliberate: civility is a character trait, a disposition focused on certain persons (political opponents). Like other virtues, civility will be better learned from examples and stories than from rules.

Stephen Carter's recent book, *Civility: Manners, Morals, and the Etiquette of Democracy*, abounds in both examples and rules. The strength of his book lies in his examples, stories of civil persons who can be admired, contrasted with cautionary stories of incivility. The weakness of Carter's book is his fifteen rules of civility[16]; this over-abundance of rules suggests that something has gone awry, unless we understand Carter's rules as pointers and helps rather than real rules. A virtue is not captured in a list of rules. Carter's many-faceted list of rules also indicates a fourth misunderstanding of civility.

4. Civility does not cover the whole territory. Carter and others make civility a virtue appropriate to any interaction between strangers, that is, people outside the circle of family and friendship. As his title, *Civility: Manners, Morals, and the Etiquette of Democracy*, suggests, he makes civility out to be a version of manners. According to Carter, civility should be practiced when neighbors move in, when meeting strangers at the market, when discussing religion, when riding trains or buses, when attending a dinner party, when campaigning for office, etc. Carter's "civility" is like "civil society" in the confusion of usages I described earlier in this chapter. Depending on which thinker you read, "civil society" includes just about every social institution; Carter's "civility" covers just about all human interactions, except family.[17] The problem is that by stretching a virtue to cover all sorts of situations, Carter makes it hard to analyze the virtue. If civility is everywhere applicable, what is it really? It's not love, nor

benevolence.   As near as I can tell, Carter's civility is a kind of generalized good will toward any stranger.

Perhaps there is a virtue to be cultivated along Carter's lines, and if people agree to call it civility, that's fine. If we do, we will need to find some other word for the virtue I am calling civility. Surely there is a virtue to be cultivated that focuses on the political foe. We are tempted to *ignore* the stranger, but we are tempted to *destroy* the political opponent. By training ourselves in civility, we will be more likely to overcome such temptation.

My complaint against Carter is not just semantic or analytical. We ought to choose our words carefully, and we should try to get our concepts clear: good philosophical goals.   But as a romantic in philosophy, I think moral philosophy should go further; it should seek to direct praxis. How can we get better? In our political lives, one thing we can do is train ourselves in civility. That training will be better focused if we see civility not as a generalized commitment to the common good or respect for all strangers, but as a disposition directed to the political opponent.

Civility, Politics and Business

I have mentioned the notion of training in civility. I want to suggest, as surprising as it will seem to some readers, that a training ground lies ready to hand for most of us—the world of business. Most adults in the United States work for large or medium sized business organizations.[18] These groups of people regularly make decisions, thus they are occasions for politics. Virtually everyone can testify that business politics produces political opponents, and the existence of political opponents calls for civility. Practicing civility in the places where we earn our livings may prepare us to be civil to opponents in other parts of our lives.

In the next chapter, I will give a more complete account of virtue as a functional characteristic and show how civility tends to produce success in business. In later chapters we will look at civility in public politics.

Notes

[1] Readers may consult the bibliography (p. 105) for a sampling of the literature.

---

[2] James Schmidt, "Is Civility a Virtue?" in *Civility*, Ed. Leroy Rouner (Notre Dame, Indiana: University of Notre Dame Press, 2000), p. 19.

[3] Schmidt, pp.18-19.

[4] See Schmidt, pp. 23-30 for a history. In the same volume, see Lawrence Cahoon, "Civic Meetings, Cultural Meanings," pp. 42-48.

[5] Benjamin Barber, *A Place for Us* (New York: Hill and Wang, 1998).

[6] Stephen L. Carter. *Civility: Manners, Morals, and the Etiquette of Democracy* (New York: Basic Books, 1998), p. 249-264.

[7] Carrie Doehring, "Civility in the Family" in *Civility*, Ed. Leroy Rouner (Notre Dame, Indiana: Notre Dame University Press, 2000), pp. 168-184.

[8] Carter, pp. 71-73, and 101-102.

[9] Barber, p. 6.

[10] In particular, I am concerned to resist the assumption made by many that moral considerations don't play in the market realm as opposed to family life or civil society. My experience with MBA students convinces me that business people desire to do right in business politics as much as citizens desire to do right in public politics.

It is relevant in this regard to reflect that the nation-state system, which we may take to be part of the natural order of things, is a recent arrival in human history. At various times and places, thoughtful people have regarded the city-state, the clan, the empire, feudalism, or other forms of government to be normal. The nation-state system is a few hundred years old, but that does not guarantee its future. One might speculate that politics on Earth in 2200 will be as different from now as the nation-state system is from medieval Europe. Perhaps, as some have speculated, international corporations will become the main players in future politics. However the form of politics changes, human beings will still have the problem of making group decisions. So I think the definition in the text goes to the heart of politics.

[11] See Mark Kingwell, *A Civil Tongue: Justice, Dialogue, and the Politics of Pluralism* (University Park, Pennsylvania: The Pennsylvania State Press, 1995). I discuss Kingwell in chapter five.

[12] Again, more on this in the next chapter. See Alasdair MacIntyre, *After Virtue*. 2nd Ed. (Notre Dame, Indiana: University of Notre Dame Press, 1984). See especially chapter 14, "The Nature of the Virtues."

[13] For examples, Washington's list gives instructions for standing by a fireplace, entering a room, dining at table, and a host of other social situations.

[14] Amy Vanderbilt, *New Complete Book of Etiquette: A Guide to Contemporary Living* (New York: Doubleday, 1952), p. xi: "Etiquette has to do with when your wear white gloves and how you unfold your napkin on your

lap; real manners are being thoughtful toward others, being creative in doing nice things for people, or sympathizing with others' problems."

[15] George Washington was still concerned about hat honor a hundred years later—though his concern was how to do it properly, not to question it.

[16] Summarized in Carter's chapter 16, "The Etiquette of Democracy."

[17] If we understand politics and civility as I have suggested, they apply to family life as much as the office or the public square.

[18] Heilbroner, Robert and Lester Thurow, *Economics Explained* (New York: Touchstone Books, 1998), pp. 45-46.

Chapter Three:

The Virtue of Civility in the Practice of Politics

This chapter has more than one goal. First, I want to introduce readers to the apparatus of practices, institutions and virtues (PIV) that helps us understand what virtues are. Second, I want to explore the notion of politics a little, to see what its main problem is. (I will claim, perhaps surprisingly, that business management is largely a variation of politics.) Third, I want to reintroduce civility and suggest that it is an important contributor to solving the political problem (and problems of management).

Throughout this chapter, I will emphasize process. As we shall see, process is integrated in more than one way into the whole structure of virtues, as we learn what virtues are and as we train ourselves in them. Already, in chapter one, I suggested that controversies are processes in which we can seek truth. The writing and reading of books constitute another process in which we can seek truth. I hope that the things I write here will contribute to a wider discussion of the virtue of civility, a discussion which may promote truth, even if the particular ideas I espouse here turn out to be wrong.

Practices, Institutions and Virtues

1. Practices. Most of what I want to say in this section is based on chapter 14, "The Nature of the Virtues," in Alasdair MacIntyre's book, *After Virtue*. Part of what MacIntyre has to say in his book is that virtues can only be understood in a socially constructed context. Virtues make sense against a background of "practices."

> By a "practice" I am going to mean any coherent and complex form of socially established cooperative human activity through which goods internal to that form of activity are realized in the course of trying to achieve those standards of excellence which are appropriate to, and partially definitive of, that form of activity, with the result that human powers to achieve excellence, and human conceptions of the ends and goods involved, are systematically extended.[1]

Note, first, that by this definition practices are complex and cooperative forms of human activity. MacIntyre says that throwing a football with skill is not a practice, but playing football is. Planting turnips is not a practice; farming is. Tic-tac-toe is not a practice, but physics, chemistry, biology, history, painting and music all are.[2]

Note also that according to the definition a practice aims at achieving "goods internal to that form of activity." An internal good is one that is made possible only by the particular practice that produces it or some other very similar practice. An external good may be gained by success in a practice, but it may also be gained in other ways. MacIntyre illustrates the difference with a story of a bright child learning to play chess. At first, the child doesn't really want to learn chess, so an adult promises a reward of a bit of candy if the child plays, and a bit more if the child wins. (The adult promises to play at a level where the child can win, but only if she plays as well as she can.) The candy motivates the child to play and to learn to play better. The candy is an external good; it is not an intrinsic part of chess, and as long as the candy alone motivates the child, the child has no reason not to win by cheating. But the adult hopes that the child will come to have other reasons for playing chess. She will discover goods that only chess makes possible: a particular kind of analytic skill, strategic imagination, competitive intensity, etc. She will come to value chess for its internal goods, and she will come to see that cheating, though it may gain her external goods, destroys the internal goods of chess.[3]

Notice, in this example, that we say the child "comes to" value chess, that she "comes to" see that cheating ruins chess. These insights don't happen all at once, no more than skill in chess is gained all at once. The beginner gains both skill and insight by a process of training in a practice.

The internal goods of a practice can only be gained through that practice (or another practice of the same type), and to a large degree they are only recognizable by people who have gained a measure of competence in the practice. Non-chess players may not recognize the internal goods of chess that motivate chess players. People without relevant experience cannot judge the internal goods of a practice.

2. Institutions. MacIntyre warns us not to confuse practices with institutions. Institutions are human organizations that grow up around a practice and make it possible. Playing chess is a practice; chess clubs, companies which publish chess literature or produce chess sets, chess clocks and other paraphernalia, and national and international chess organizations are all institutions.

Institutions control external goods related to practices. Typically, external goods include money, prestige, and status. But institutions cannot control the internal goods of a practice. Chess institutions can recognize so-and-so as a master level player; they can award a prize to so-and-so as winner of some competition; and they can declare so-and-so to be city, regional, national or world champion. But chess institutions are unable to give anyone the internal goods peculiar to a well-played game.

Because institutions control external goods but not internal goods, MacIntyre points out that institutions are always susceptible to "corruption." An institution becomes corrupt to the extent that it so focuses attention on external goods that it fails to enable the relevant practice to achieve internal goods. When the participants in a practice focus their attention on external goods of money and prestige granted by some institution, the practice in which they engage and the goods internal to that practice may suffer. Consider an artist who paints, sings, dances, or acts to achieve fame or wealth rather than excellence. External goods and internal goods may be achieved together, but in some cases they are incompatible; the virtues that enable one to gain the goods internal to the practice may prevent one from gaining external goods.[4] (E.g., the honesty of a really good lawyer may prevent her from winning certain external rewards, but the internal goods of a practice of law cannot be had without that honesty.)

Institutions may be short-lived, such as a weekend chess tournament; they may endure as organizations far longer than any of the human beings involved in them, as with professional or scientific associations like the American Medical Association.

What we call business is not a single practice, though we might think of business as a group of practices. Retailing clothing is a practice, as is producing beverages, providing nursing care, and thousands of other businesses. Each of these practices is a complex, cooperative human endeavor that has its own internal standards of excellence. Each of them exists to achieve internal goods made possible only by the practice. Through the institutions associated with these practices we also gain external goods, money in particular. We often focus on the external rewards of a job, but if that is all there is to a job—if there are no internal goods achieved by anyone involved—then the activity ceases to be a practice. And it's probably dehumanizing.

3. Virtues. With a description of practices and institutions in place, MacInyre can give an initial definition of virtues.

> A virtue is an acquired human quality the possession of which tends to enable us to achieve those goods which are internal to practices and the lack of which effectively prevents us from achieving any such goods.[5]

Note, here, that virtues are acquired characteristics. MacIntyre's definition rules out things such as natural physical strength or beauty. However much these things are prized, they are not moral virtues. Acquiring a quality requires a process of learning or training. Beginners in some practice may not have the virtues necessary for success in that practice, and one measure of their increasing success in the practice will be their acquisition of the relevant virtues.

Now, to engage in a practice means to submit to an ongoing human activity (that is, unless one were to invent a totally new practice on one's own). Beginners don't get to do just anything they like and call it architecture or gardening. Beginners have to learn the practice, and this involves learning its skills, procedures, and standards of excellence. Once the beginner has become competent in the practice, she may challenge some of the methods and standards of the practice, but only after she has gained a measure of expertise in the practice as she inherited it. All practices have histories, and the skills and standards of a practice evolve over time. In learning and participating in a practice, the beginner involves herself in a community-through-time defined by that practice.

It is already clear, says MacIntyre, that some virtues are needed in all practices: justice, courage, and honesty.[6] If the standards of excellence in some practice are not applied justly (suppose a teacher granted grades on the basis of personal appearance), the internal goods of the practice are undermined. (There are internal goods to the practice of education, and students need just feedback to improve.) For a practice to adapt over time, some of its practitioners have to challenge some of its methods and standards, and it takes courage to suggest that we think and act in new ways. Without at least a minimal level of honesty, people cannot cooperate in a practice at all.

To be sure, some people engage in practices with little virtue (and much vice). By their lack of courage, justice or honesty, they may gain many external goods—and external goods are real goods, so we can understand why vice is tempting. But such people are, in a sense, free riders. They are parasitical on the system. At least some people engaged in a practice must exhibit at least some level of courage, honesty, and justice, or else the practice will cease to produce the internal goods for which it exists.

Courage, honesty, and justice are not the only virtues, obviously. Perhaps every practice needs other "acquired human qualities" to achieve its internal goods. Readers are free to imagine the acquired characteristics that enable success in the practices with which they are familiar.

One more aspect of the structure of practices, institutions and virtues must be mentioned. As MacInyre defines them, virtues depend on practices. But what about evil human practices? Should we say that the "acquired human qualities" which helped produce "success" in the complex and cooperative human endeavor known as Auschwitz were "virtues"? We recognize that Nazi soldiers were brave, but does that make their courage right?[7]

MacIntyre's answer lies in the notion of *telos*. A telos of a thing is the purpose or goal for which it exists. Every practice has a telos, and it is by pursuing that goal that people gain the internal goods of the practice. At first, a beginner may not have a good grasp of the purpose of a practice; he may participate mainly to gain external goods. After a while, as he participates in institutions that maintain the practice and gains skills and virtues necessary for success in the practice, the telos becomes more clear to him.

The notion of telos applies not just to practices, but also to a person's whole life. Here MacIntyre defends an Aristotelian view of things. We must ask: what is the purpose (telos) of a human life? It is possible that we could come to the conclusion that some practices are incompatible with a good life.

Remember process here. The competent practitioners of some practice may disagree over the precise formulation of the goal of their practice. Consider driving. In a class exercise I have sometimes suggested that the purpose of driving is "safe and timely arrival." But other competent drivers—there are millions of us—say that driving is also about having fun. We need not reach final agreement about the telos of driving to recognize that some attitudes and behaviors of drivers partake of vice (tailgating, inattentiveness, etc.) while others are virtues (e.g. patience). Part of what it means to engage in a practice is to engage in the debate over the goals and standards of excellence of that practice. The practice evolves over time.

In the same way, MacIntyre suggests that a healthy community would involve its members in a debate over the details of the good life. In fact, part of the good life is the search for the good life, and some virtues are virtues because they help us sustain that search.[8] A healthy community would continue to debate just what the proper human telos is, but it could exclude certain things as inimical to the human telos, even broadly understood. People who are reasonably competent in the practice of political philosophy can agree that running concentration camps is not compatible with the good life, even if they are still arguing over how to best understand the good life.

The Problem of Politics

To begin, recall the definition of "politics" I offered in the last chapter; politics is the art or science of making decisions for groups of people. Thus defined, politics includes family politics, university politics, business politics, church politics, and governmental politics from small town meetings to the U.S. Congress or the U.N. General Assembly. Whenever a group of people needs to decide what they believe or what they will do, the political problem emerges.

The political problem has to do with conflict. As the joke goes (which I have heard told about Quakers and other groups), where two or three are gathered, there are three or four opinions. People often do not agree about what they believe, or about what to do. So political decisions must be made in the context of conflict, and it is often thought, wrongly, that political decisions ought to eliminate conflict.

The goal of politics can't be the elimination of conflict, because some conflict helps produce better decisions for the people involved. Many writers on business management have pointed out that in some circumstances, lack of conflict causes as much difficulty as too much conflict. Decision-making bodies afflicted with "group think" have too little conflict. Everyone in the group sees the question before them in similar ways, so each one readily agrees to the first policy proposal offered, and other, possibly better, solutions are not considered. Wise leaders will sometimes deliberately foster conflicting views in the decision making body—as when a conservative president includes liberals in his cabinet, or vice versa—in order to produce more creative thinking, and thus better decisions.

If the goal of politics isn't the elimination of conflict, what is it? On a superficial level, I just identified the goal of politics as "better decisions." But what are better decisions? How do we tell good political decisions from bad ones? How do we tell good political decisions from even better ones? We are asking what the telos of politics is.

I suggest that the telos of politics is *shalom*. This biblical Hebrew word means "peace," but also much more. It involves harmony, completeness, integrity, and wholeness. In a community of shalom no one starves, because shalom includes physical contentedness. In a community of shalom no one despairs, because shalom includes psychological health. In a community of shalom no one faces his problems alone, because shalom includes solidarity. And so on.[9]

Clearly, in using shalom to describe the political telos, I am describing a goal toward which we move, not something that any society has achieved. Remember what was said earlier about the process of understanding the good life. We do not simply turn to our pastor or rabbi or professor to tell us what shalom means (though we should listen eagerly to what his or her expertise might teach us); all of us who competently participate in politics participate also in the debate about the goal of politics. Part of the good life is discovering what the good life is; part of shalom is discovering what shalom is. We engage in the process of discovery as members of an ongoing community, inheriting central ideas from previous generations, but reforming those ideas in a continual search for truth.

As we search together to understand shalom and move toward it, I think we will find that some conflict is necessary to shalom. A variety of views, vigorously promoted, makes conflict. Out of that conflict comes creativity and new options, options that none of the parties to the conflict had considered. Sometimes, only creative options will move us toward shalom.

Of course, I hardly need to say that some conflict, or the way we handle some conflict, is destructive. Practices of all sorts—gardening, commodity trading, clothing manufacture, research in organic chemistry, etc.—depend on institutions to sustain them. All those institutions provide situations for politics. And all of those institutions are susceptible to destructive conflict, usually as people pursue external goods.[10]   Sometimes the institution itself is destroyed, and sometimes the institution continues while the practice involved is reduced to producing merely external goods. More importantly, sometimes the conflict destroys people.

One could say that the theoretical problem of moral philosophy in regard to politics is distinguishing destructive conflicts from constructive conflicts. (One might even go so far as to put it this way: distinguishing loving conflict from hateful conflict. But this would sidetrack our discussion with complications.[11]) The practical problem of politics is to respond to conflict in ways that contribute to shalom rather than reduce it. How do we conduct our controversies in ways that move us toward truth?

The institutions that most dominate our lives—our businesses, schools, churches, and governments—all exist to sustain practices. In all these institutions we must deal with conflict. If we handle conflict well, the institutions will better sustain the practices and the internal goods at which they aim. So I suggest that the principle problem of business management is a political problem, the management of conflict.

The Virtue of Civility in the Practice of Politics

Remember MacIntyre's definition of a virtue: "an acquired human quality the possession of which tends to enable us to achieve those goods which are internal to practices and the lack of which effectively prevents us from achieving any such goods."

Now I want to suggest that politics, as defined in the previous chapter—the art or science of making decisions for groups of people—is a practice.[12] We might call it a "second level" practice, since people engage in it in the service of institutions which themselves exist to sustain "first level" practices.

Illustration: a pharmacist engages in the first level practice of providing pharmacological services to the public. He gains external rewards (income, local recognition) and achieves internal goods (at which I can only guess) which pharmacists know. He participates in several institutions that sustain the practice of pharmacy: his own store, a drug supply cooperative, and a state pharmacists' association. In each of these institutions he joins others in making group decisions; he participates in the second level practice of politics. Perhaps he participates in politics only for external goods (he wants recognition by HMOs for his store), but he may also gain goods internal to the political process (a sense of empowerment, perhaps, or a feeling that he has defended his values by urging the pharmacists' association to oppose assisted suicide).

I suppose there are many virtues (acquired characteristics which tend to enable acquisition of internal goods) of politics: courage, honesty, justice, creativity, hope, practical judgment, etc. Among these virtues is civility.

Remember from the last chapter the definition of civility I suggested. Civility is *a properly grounded character trait that moves an individual to treat political opponents well and/or to feel certain emotions toward political opponents, emotions that move an individual to treat political opponents well.* A few comments on this definition will help make it clearer.[13] First, civility is directed toward one's political opponents; I suppose we should be civil to our political allies as well, but that's easier. Second, civility moves us to treat our political opponents "well"; that is, we shouldn't impugn their motives, lie about them, use *ad-hominem* or other fallacious arguments against them, or ignore them; and we should keep our agreements with them, debate honestly with them, and respect them. Third, civility is a character trait, not merely an action or collection of actions. Civility, as other virtues, describes who a person is, not just what she does. Last, note that civility is "properly grounded"; this requires explanation.

Virtues have to do not just with a person's observable actions, but also his motivations for those actions. Aristotle illustrated the point by imagining different soldiers, all standing in battle line, doing what a brave man does, but each exhibiting some kind of pseudo-courage. For instance, the ignorant man fought with no understanding that battles could be dangerous, the professional soldier fought because he was experienced and calculating, and the citizen soldier fought to achieve recognition from his fellow citizens. None of these men, Aristotle said, exhibited true courage. In a similar way, I imagine that people could treat their political opponents well for the wrong reasons. Perhaps, like the ignorant soldier, they don't understand that civility has its dangers. Or, like the professional soldier, they calculate that treating one's opponent well is the best way to achieve their goals. These sorts of civility will wilt in certain circumstances—when the cost of civility becomes apparent, when treating an opponent well may produce political defeat.

Now, just what the proper ground for civility is is not the subject of this chapter.[14]   Process again: while still pressing for agreement about the basis for civility, we can agree that it describes an important virtue, and we can explore the ways it tends toward achieving the internal goods of politics. There are at least four advantages which civility contributes to the practice of politics.

First, civility helps prevent destructive conflict. Remember the plaintive words of Rodney King, after the acquittal of the police officers who beat him and the riot that followed. "People, I just want to say, you know, can we all get along? . . . I mean, we're all stuck here for a while. Let's try to work it out."[15]   Riots show us how destructive conflict can be; surely we want to avoid *that*. But political conflict with less fury and on a smaller scale (maybe it is "only" verbal, on a work team or at town council) can still be destructive of institutions and the practices institutions sustain.

Second, civility helps preserve participants in a political process as resources for decision-making. An important turn comes when we stop seeing the political opponent as merely an obstacle or a naysayer and see the opponent as a resource for better decision-making. My political opponent sees the issue differently than I do. He may have information or values or concerns that I don't know about. (I may think I already know all about his reasons for opposing my position, but I probably don't.) If I treat my opponent well, his knowledge, values, and concerns remain available as resources for inventing new options. If I have the power to do so, and if I cut my opponent out of the decision process, I effectively reduce my resources for making a good decision.

Third, civility helps reduce distortions in communication. Political processes, whether the institution is a hospital or computer chip company, depend on communication. Nothing fouls up communication quite as effectively as enmity. It breeds fear, mistrust, lies, and manipulation. But the virtue of civility expresses itself in treating opponents well. This feature of civility is so important that people have invented rules of order and etiquette (sometimes formally adopted in written form) to preserve it. Rules, though, are not enough; we need the actual virtue, the character trait which motivates proper behavior.

Fourth, civility helps preserve participants in politics as people of dignity. Which is more important, defeating Mrs. Brown's silly proposal to paint the church nursery walls brown, or treating Mrs. Brown herself as a person of worth? A civil person may oppose Mrs. Brown's ideas, but he will do so without opposing Mrs. Brown.

The practice of politics is only one part of a person's life. This last advantage of civility looks beyond politics and connects a person's character as a political actor with her character in the whole of life. If we limit ourselves to the confines of a single practice, politics, the political opponent is a priceless resource, so civility is a virtue. In the context of one's whole life, the political opponent turns out to be a human being, worthy of even more respect, so this fourth advantage of civility is most important of all.

A Caution

We should be clear-minded about the costs of civility. A candidate who treats his opponent well may lose the election. (Attack ads, especially when delivered on television late in an election campaign, are distressingly successful. Nevertheless, the civil candidate will eschew them.) A university that treats other schools fairly may see them gain students at its expense. A mid-level manager who treats other managers in his firm well may lose rewards and prestige to an unscrupulous colleague.

In short: if you treat your opponent well, he might beat you. He might not be interested in better decisions. He might treat politics as a win-lose proposition. You can invite him to participate in politics more competently—that is, more virtuously—but there are people who have not been well trained in politics and who seem to think its telos is winning. You may find training such people in the true purpose of politics a long, difficult business.

Nevertheless, I contend that civility is a real virtue. If we cultivate it in ourselves, we will more readily reap the internal goods of politics. We will make progress toward shalom.

Notes

[1] Alasdair MacIntyre, *After Virtue* 2nd ed. (Notre Dame, Indiana: University of Notre Dame Press, 1984), p. 187.

[2] MacIntyre, p. 187.

[3] MacIntyre, p. 188.

[4] MacIntyre, p. 196.

[5] MacIntyre, p. 191.

[6] MacIntyre, p. 191.

[7] MacIntyre, p. 200.

[8] MacIntrye, p. 219.

[9] Biblical scholars have much to say about shalom. For example, see Gerhard von Rad, *Old Testament Theology*, Vol. 1 (New York: Harper & Row, 1962), p. 130.

[10] Can people fall into destructive conflict over the internal goods of a practice? One might argue that truly internal goods of a practice are available to anyone competent in that practice, so no forced choice, win-lose, situations need arise. (E.g. only one or a few researchers will get the Nobel Prize in chemistry, but all the researchers can experience the internal goods of chemistry. The Nobel Prize is an external good.) Conversely, some practices might be like competitive games, where some of the internal goods of the practice are available to only some of the people involved. Fortunately, we don't need to resolve this interesting debate to move on. It's safe to say most destructive conflict arises over external goods.

[11] "Can the conflict be assigned a loving or hateful label, or only the actions of the participants? If all parties are hateful, is the conflict hateful? . . . Is a loving conflict the same as a constructive conflict?"—Bennet Smith, private communication.

[12] One might object that making decisions in a state legislature is far different from making decisions in a family. So rather than speaking of the practice of politics, perhaps I ought to refer to many different but related practices of politics. But even if there are many different varieties of politics, we can treat them as one in this context, because civility will be a virtue in them all.

[13] For a fuller discussion, see chapter two.

[14] See chapter six, "A Basis for Civility."

[15] *Life Magazine*, June 1992.

Chapter Four:

Robert Audi's Rules for Civility

(And Why They Don't Work)

In earlier chapters, I invited the reader to think about the way we conduct controversies, and I suggested that "civility" names a virtue which will help us succeed in our controversies—that is, if "success" in a controversy is finding truth, better decisions, and/or shalom. In this chapter and the following chapter we will focus on controversies in public politics, a subset of all the controversies in which civility is needed, but an instructive subset. Naturally, we find more written by political philosophers about public politics than any other group decision-making process. In examining a tiny sampling of political philosophy, I may seem to lose track of civility as discussed so far. My foray into political philosophy will be justified, though, if it produces a deeper understanding of civility by tying that concept to wider philosophical ideas.

I am a voter in Oregon, a state that has a long history of the use of the initiative process. Since the early 1900s, voters in Oregon have made direct electoral decisions about issues as diverse as taxes, parochial education, land use planning, and civil rights for homosexuals. Oregon's liberal initiative process allows citizens to bring proposals for new statutes and even constitutional amendments before the electorate with relative ease.

I am also a Christian, trying to live in a way consonant with my faith. How should I, someone trying to live faithfully as a Christian, think about my responsibilities as a voter in Oregon? My case is only an illustration of the general problem: How should religious belief affect the way the believer votes?

Robert Audi has given some thought to the intersection of faith and public policy and has offered guidelines that are relevant to my question.[1] Audi's topic is Christian citizenship. He does not use the language of "virtues" or "civility," and he offers rules or principles. Remember that in chapter two I suggested that civility, like other virtues, is a matter of character rather than rules. Nevertheless, Audi clearly is concerned about our topic: how to conduct controversies. It is easy to see how his principles, if they are right, should shape our concept of civility. In this chapter I will illustrate and test his principles by two examples. I hope to show appreciation for the wisdom of Audi's advice, while also suggesting why I think his principles fail to solve the problem of Christian citizenship and thus fail to accurately describe civility. Before discussion of my examples, I will review Audi's main points.

Two Rules for Religious Argument in Liberal Democracies

The context for my question, as Audi points out, is liberal democracy, which, among other values, prizes religious liberty. "Liberal democracies are free societies and are above all committed to preserving freedom, especially in religion," Audi notes.[2] Now, the political theory of liberal democracy must at least meet what Audi calls a "fidelity to essential premises constraint," that is, democratic duties must at least include those commitments which are necessary to maintaining democracy. Since liberal democracies prize religious freedom, our political theory should endorse commitments needed to sustain religious freedom.[3]

Audi says that one such commitment must be the ideal of personal autonomy, in the sense of self-determination. I agree. It is hard to see how a society could prize religious liberty without also prizing the right of individuals to believe and act as they choose, at least in regard to religious beliefs and activities. Audi suggests that the ideal of autonomy alone will produce important guidelines for the religious citizen-voter.

> It seems to me that once autonomy is taken sufficiently seriously—as it will be not only by liberal theorists but also by any sound moral theory—the way is open to view the justification of coercion in a framework that gives high priority to respect for the self-determination of persons. For purposes of sociopolitical philosophy, it may be fruitful to work from a *surrogacy conception of justified coercion*, especially in cases of governmental coercion.[4]

Note that here coercion first comes up as an important term in our discussion of civility. Chapter eight will give closer attention to the question of coercion—that is, when is it right to coerce other people?—but we cannot avoid it entirely until then. Audi's "surrogacy conception of justified coercion," which he explains in some detail, implies at a minimum that "we may coerce people to do only what they would autonomously do if appropriately informed and fully rational."[5] Audi claims that citizens in liberal democracies will not resent proper laws that restrict their freedom, for once the rationale for the coercion is explained, citizens will agree to the law. Coercion based on some rationale (even if it is correct) that is inaccessible to a rational informed person will tend to cause resentment in that person. And, says Audi,

> . . . it is part of the underlying rationale of liberalism that we should not have to feel this kind of resentment—that we give up autonomy only where, no matter what our specific preferences or particular world view, we can be expected, given adequate rationality and sufficient information, to see that we would have so acted on our own.[6]

Arguments for coercion based on religious revelation have rationales inaccessible to unbelievers, so they would resent such coercion. Other limitations on coercion would go beyond this minimum. For instance, even if a fully rational and informed person—for purely rational reasons—would worship God, the ideal of autonomy precludes coercing her to so worship. Audi says there may be other areas of life in which liberal society protects one's freedom to decline even what reason requires.[7]

Given these implications of the ideal of autonomy, Audi says that the main basis of sociopolitical decisions should be "secular reasons," that is, reasons "whose normative force does not evidentially depend on the existence of God or on theological considerations, or on the pronouncements of a person or institution qua religious authority."[8] The religious person's political conduct should be governed by two principles:

> . . .the *principle of secular rationale* says that one has a prima facie obligation not to advocate or support any law or public policy that restricts human conduct unless one has, and is willing to offer, adequate secular reason for this advocacy or support.

> . . .the *principle of secular motivation* adds the idea that one also has a prima facie obligation to abstain from such advocacy or support unless one is sufficiently *motivated* by adequate secular reason.[9]

A clarification: Audi says that persons have a political right to argue and vote on religious bases; he is interested in an "ought" that goes beyond this political right. He is interested in the ideal to which the Christian citizen can aspire. At this point Audi comes closest to thinking about citizenship in terms of virtue rather than act theory.

A further clarification: in addition to secular reasons for some public policy, Audi says a religious person may have religious reasons for that policy which she thinks evidentially stronger than her secular reasons, and she may actually be more strongly motivated by those religious reasons than by her secular reasons. Audi's principles only ask a religious person to (1) restrict herself to sufficient secular reason when trying to persuade, and (2) support only those policies she *would* support *if* her only motivation were secular.

I wish to examine these principles by means of two examples.

The Racist

Imagine a voter in a state not unlike Oregon in a time not unlike the late 1800s, when Jim Crow laws were implemented in many states. A voter in such a state would have opportunity to vote, through the initiative process, on all sorts of public issues, including matters of race relations.

The voter we are imagining holds strong views on the proper relationship between races. He reads in his Bible (Genesis 9:24-27) how Noah blessed his sons Shem and Japheth and cursed his grandson Canaan, saying, "May Canaan be the slave of Shem." This voter believes, since he has been taught by authoritative voices in his church, that this divine blessing and cursing applied not just to Shem and Canaan, but also to all their descendants, establishing a permanent order for human societies. The voter further believes, having been taught by his church, that Shem represents white Europeans and Canaan represents black Africans. In divine ordering, then, blacks are by nature to be subservient to whites. In short, the voter we are imagining is a religious racist, a person whose racist beliefs are supported by religious beliefs.

We imagine that the racist has grudgingly accepted the outcome of the civil war, the end of slavery in the United States. But he continues to believe that whites are in fact better than blacks, and he believes society should maintain the dominant position of whites over blacks whenever possible.

Imagine further that in this year's election, our racist has the opportunity to vote on a miscegenation initiative. Some citizens of his state, horrified by the "scandal" of a black man married to a white woman, have put an initiative on the ballot which would forbid their state to grant marriage licenses to mixed race couples. Given our imagined religious racist's views, we are not surprised that he intends to vote yes.

Our racist's vote represents evil religion intruding into politics. It is the sort of thing many secularists have in mind when they decry religion's presence in the public square. Audi's rules for the religious person's participation in politics are supposed to help us with such examples.

What should we say about our racist's beliefs? Especially if we are religious people ourselves, we might want to correct the way his religion supports his racist beliefs by objecting to his outrageous misuse of the Bible, his impious misunderstanding of the nature of God, or his bizarre sociological ideas. Audi's rules don't take this approach. They don't ask the racist to change his religious beliefs, no matter how egregious they are, but they ask him to *justify by secular reasons any public action that restricts the freedom of others.* Further, Audi's rules ask that the religious person be *sufficiently motivated by secular reasons*, so that he not use secular arguments as a front for a purely religious concern.

If Audi's principles are right, clearly they are relevant to civility as we have been discussing it. The civil person, I have said, is motivated to treat her political opponent well. Audi's rules give a certain twist to the notion of treating an opponent well, by restricting the kinds of reasons the civil person will use to justify freedom-restricting policies.

Audi's first rule asks the racist to justify his vote for the measure forbidding interracial marriage with adequate secular reasons. Clearly, he will not be able to do this, since there are no adequate reasons to support invidious racism.[10] So, even if he feels strongly as a matter of religious belief that he ought to vote yes, by Audi's rules the racist ought either to vote no or abstain from voting.[11]

The attraction of Audi's rules becomes apparent. They let us see that the racist's views ought not to be enacted into liberty-restricting laws without requiring us to refute those views. The racist is entitled to believe what he likes, but as a good citizen in a liberal democracy he must only urge those policies he can adequately defend on secular, "neutral" grounds. Audi's position illustrates a familiar principle in political philosophy, the priority of right over good.[12] This opens the possibility, bright with hope, that we can be good citizens without first resolving religious differences amongst us. After Europe's religious wars in the seventeenth century, this possibility of political civility (among other things) attracted people to enlightenment philosophy in the eighteenth century.[13]

Having an appreciation for the wisdom of Audi's rules, I want to test them by another example.

The Pacifist

Again imagine a voter in a state not unlike Oregon, with a liberal initiative process, but this time with no close tie to other states or to a federal government. Such a voter would be able to vote on foreign policy and national defense issues, since no outside government would exist to set policy for the state.

This voter has strong beliefs about how states ought to relate to each other. She is a pacifist. She thinks all wars and war making are wrong. Our pacifist is not deterred from her pacifist convictions by the various arguments of her friends that some war making is just, partly for historical reasons. (The fact that her government declares its war making to be just is hardly reassuring. At most half of such governmental claims could possibly be right, and in practice far fewer than half are judged as just, even by just war theorists.) But the fundamental reason our pacifist rejects all war is religious.

The pacifist believes that Jesus is the savior of the world, that in him God reaches out to rebellious humanity with mercy and forgiveness. She thinks that Jesus is also the "Lord," that is, one who has the right to command human beings. On the basis of Jesus' commands to love and pray for one's enemies, she rejects the jingoism and hatred that accompany war. On the basis of Jesus' cross, she believes that *this* is the way that God reconciles the world to himself, through redemptive suffering. On the basis of Jesus' resurrection, she trusts that in spite of all apparent defeats, the way of the cross will be ultimately vindicated.

Imagine that in this political year a crisis has been brewing between the pacifist's state and a neighboring state. The President-for-Life of the neighboring state has accused the pacifist's state of violating economic treaties between the states. His charges have been increasingly bellicose, and many citizens in our pacifist's state are concerned that they need to prepare collective defense. They have placed a measure on the ballot that authorizes an increase in the army and levies a poll tax to pay for it.

Our imagined pacifist wants to be a good citizen. What considerations should rule her thinking as she prepares to vote on the proposed war-preparations law?

Someone might argue that a vote in favor of the war-preparations act could be consistent with pursuing peace. This is the familiar argument that the best way to prevent war is to so effectively prepare for it that no one will attack you. But it seems that for a deterrent threat to be effective, a state must convincingly express the willingness to use the deterrent, a policy inconsistent with pacifism.[14]

The pacifist might think that since God, through Christ's teaching, death and resurrection, has forbidden her to participate in war, she should vote against the war bill. Audi would say she is within her rights to vote against the war bill, but that is not to say she should. Can she give *secular* reasons against the war-preparation initiative?

On a piecemeal basis the pacifist could give secular arguments against most war-preparation measures. Though constructed in countless ways, these arguments boil down to the fundamental secular anti-war argument, that the evils of the war itself would outweigh the evils the war was supposed to prevent.

But assume that we are imagining an unusual case. Our pacifist's state is a peace loving society. Its war aims are defensive. Many citizens believe that the President-for-Life of the neighboring state is a monstrous tyrant, and they worry that his invasion, if not stopped, will become genocide. In short, our imagined pacifist may have a hard time coming up with secular reasons to oppose *this* war, at least as it is conceived by her fellow citizens in the period before the war.

The pacifist may suspect that the information upon which she and her fellow citizens must make their decision is tainted, biased or less than the full story. It is the nature of news media to deal in crises and simplistic analysis of crises. And there are people, sometimes serving in government, who fan the flames of bellicosity by deliberately skewing the information citizens have about other countries. Perhaps if she knew the whole story, the pacifist could make a good secular argument against this war—but she doesn't have the whole story, and she cannot get it before she must vote.

The pacifist is convinced, on religious grounds, that *all* wars are wrong.[15]   Let us assume, as seems likely, that no sound secular argument can be made that forbids all wars.[16]   Even if there is such an argument, our pacifist may not be able to discover it. It seems that on Audi's account we are to conclude that though the pacifist would be within her rights to vote against war-preparation, she really ought to vote yes or abstain. But if she votes yes or abstains, she makes it easier for what she must regard as an evil policy to be enacted.

A Dilemma

This result, that forces the pacifist to choose between the obligations of conscience and what she really ought to do, should trouble us. I present the case of the pacifist as a challenge, in the form of the dilemma, to Audi's rules. If Audi's principles are right, they require the pacifist either to vote against her conscience (because conscience tells her all wars are wrong) or do less than what she really ought (because she really ought to vote for the war preparations measure or abstain). If they require her to vote against her conscience, Audi's rules are defective. And if they require her to do less than what she really ought, Audi's rules are defective. Either way, Audi's rules are defective. How might Audi respond to this dilemma?

One response might try denying that there is a dilemma, like this. Since Audi's rules apply to proposed policies that limit others' autonomy, they would not apply to a pacifist who just *withdrew* from the war making of others. By absenting herself from war making, the pacifist would not limit others from engaging in whatever war making they deemed necessary.[17]

But this response will not work. In the example we have imagined, the pacifist must vote for or against the war preparations measure.[18]   If she votes in accord with her conscience, she will be doing something to limit her fellow citizens' freedom to arm themselves.[19]   She would do even more to limit their freedom if she were to campaign against the measure, if only by telling her friends her true opinion of it.[20]

Stanley Hauerwas has written, "In fact . . . there is *no* morality that does not require others to suffer for our commitments."[21]   This is a sweeping generalization, but I suspect it may be true. If it is true, then every morality will limit the autonomy of others at some point, since people rarely choose to suffer for others' commitments. If the pacifist tries to vote her morality, she will cause others to suffer, at least in the sense of preventing them from doing what they would prefer.

Another response would challenge part of the dilemma. The pacifist's conscience is an ill-formed conscience, this respondent might say. One cannot have a conscientious duty to do less than what one really ought to do. Since the pacifist admits that she cannot give adequate secular reasons to vote against the war-preparations initiative, she ought to give up her belief that it is her conscientious duty to oppose the initiative.

This response fails because it deprives Audi's rules of the wisdom that we recognized in them in the case of the racist. There, remember, we admired Audi's rules because they would prevent the racist from voting his beliefs without asking him to abandon his beliefs. But now it seems that Audi's principles require the pacifist to change her religious beliefs. Those beliefs require her to be a peacemaker, but without a secular reason for such beliefs, Audi's principles dictate that she should abet war making, or at least not oppose it.

The last option is to abandon Audi's principles; it is to say the pacifist really should follow her conscience even though she does not have (or is not motivated by) adequate secular reasons to do so. If we adopt this option, as I suggest we should, then we should notice the cost: it turns out that Audi's rules, which seemed to be wise, don't adequately describe civility. Offering and being motivated by secular reasons for freedom-limiting policies is neither a sufficient nor necessary condition of treating political opponents well.

We should note that the "pacifist dilemma" could be paralleled by a "racist dilemma." The racist's conscientious beliefs also require him to do other than what he really should, if what he really should do depends on secular reasons. The racist's beliefs are repugnant, while I, at least, find the pacifist's beliefs admirable—but this contrast should not blind us to the fact that they have the same logical relationship to Audi's principles.

On the whole it seems that Audi's best response to the pacifist dilemma is to brazen it out. He should say: The pacifist and the racist are not asked to abandon their beliefs; they are free to hold them, and even to vote on them. But if they want to do what is really right as citizens of a liberal democracy, they must not vote as they would like unless they have and are motivated by adequate secular reasons. This implies that one could believe that one has a conscientious duty to do other than what one believes one really ought to do—which sounds, and I think is, incoherent.

Audi might try to rescue his principles by noting that the rules say only that one has *prima facie* duties of secular rationale and secular motivation. Perhaps he means to imply that in some situations other factors may override these duties. Then his principles might become for-the-most-part useful advices. As such, I think they are unobjectionable. But Audi gives no word about what these other factors might be, and it is hard to imagine what other factors would allow us to say that the racist ought not to vote his conscience while the pacifist should—unless those factors include the truth or falsity of one or the other set of beliefs.

Therefore, though I am attracted to Audi's work as a way to think through my problems as a voter in Oregon, I cannot endorse his principles except as advices. I aspire to be a civil citizen of a liberal democracy. That requires that I value freedom for others and myself, and it requires that I learn civility. But, as I will argue in the next chapter, civility cannot be reduced to the demands of right; it must be based on the good.

Notes

[1] See Robert Audi, "The Place of Religious Argument in a Free and Democratic Society." *San Diego Law Review.* Vol. 30, No. 4 (Fall, 1993): 677-702.

[2] Audi, p. 687.

[3] Since they are committed to other ideals in addition to religious liberty, liberal democracies will need political theory that includes whatever commitments are necessary for those ideals as well. An obvious example: liberal political theory must prize commitments that imply one vote for each person, since democratic ideals are essential to liberal democracies. However, since I want to ask how a religious person, a Christian, should think about his political responsibilities, it will be satisfyingly elegant to define those political responsibilities in terms of religious freedom. As a Christian I certainly want the political system to protect my liberty to believe and to act as a believing person.

[4] Audi, p. 688.

[5] Audi, p. 689. I will criticize this notion, which Audi shares with many philosophers, in chapter eight.

[6] Audi, p. 690.

[7] Audi, pp. 689-690, fn. 12.

[8] Audi, p. 692.

[9] Audi, pp. 691-92.

[10] Note that the second rule does not come into play, since the racist's intended vote does not pass the first rule.

[11] I suspect that Audi would interpret his rules as saying that one should oppose measures that restrict freedom if they do not have adequate secular grounding. But since this is not clear in his paper, I interpret broadly and say that the racist should at least abstain.

[12] See chapter five for a discussion.

[13] See chapter six.

[14] Arguments of this kind swirled around the Catholic bishops' letter on nuclear weapons in the 1980s. Use of weapons of mass destruction violates just war theory. Does this fact also preclude deterrence based on the *threat* of using weapons of mass destruction? Some Catholics argued that it doesn't. But it is hard to see how a nation could maintain a credible threat to use nuclear weapons if it secretly did not intend to use them. But if using nuclear weapons is unjust, then intending to use them is unjust—on the principle that it is never right to intend wrong.

[15] Compare the testimony of early Quakers: "That Spirit of Christ by which we are guided is not changeable, so as once to command us from a thing as evil, and again to move unto it; and we do certainly know and so testify to the world, that the Spirit of Christ, which leads us into all Truth, will never move us to fight and war against any man with outward weapons, neither for the kingdom of Christ, nor for the kingdoms of this world." *The Journal of George Fox.* Ed. John L. Nickals (London: London Yearly Meeting, 1975), pp. 399-400.

[16] Since all wars includes those which have not yet been fought—a very large class of wars, whose occasions and natures we can't know—secular arguments condemning all of them would require quite general premises which would be at least as controversial as pacifism.

[17] The provisions for conscientious objector status in U.S. selective service law from 1941-1973 fit with this reasoning. COs could be tolerated as long as they did not hinder the overall war effort.

[18] She could abstain from the vote, but this makes passage of what she must regard as evil legislation more likely than if she voted against it. Abstaining from voting, in a democracy, is a morally charged act.

[19] See the discussion of voting as coercion in chapter eight.

[20] I have constructed the example, in part, just to achieve this result. But lest the reader think that the example is purely imaginary, consider the dilemma of Quaker legislators in eighteenth century Pennsylvania. For a long while the

Quaker faction controlled the colonial legislature. They were pacifists. But many non-Quaker citizens of Pennsylvania (and the British Crown) wanted the colony to defend itself by raising a militia. For a time, Quaker legislators resorted to subterfuge, voting moneys "for the King's use," and claiming no responsibility for what that use was. Eventually, such hypocrisy had to die; the Quaker legislators resigned and left the government of the colony to their non-pacifist successors. (A few abandoned pacifism and stayed in office.) Of course, if colonial Pennsylvania had had the initiative process, even this withdrawal from the dilemma would have failed.

[21] Stanley Hauerwas, *The Peaceable Kingdom* (Notre Dame, Indiana: University of Notre Dame Press, 1983), p. 9.

Chapter Five:

Civil Speech, the Right and the Good

Robert Audi doesn't expressly use "virtue" language when writing about Christian citizenship, though the principles he produces are clearly relevant to our discussion of the virtue of civility. In this chapter I will turn to a book by Mark Kingwell, *A Civil Tongue*[1], which does talk about virtue and civility.

Most of what I will say in this chapter consists of criticisms of two of Kingwell's positions, but my criticism of Kingwell on these matters should not hide the fact that I agree with him on several points. Kingwell recognizes the importance of civility to political philosophy; in fact, he goes so far as to suggest that justice—the time honored central concept of political philosophy—might simply be whatever results from a civil public dialogue. Kingwell turns to etiquette studies for material to enrich his notion of civil speech, and, though I distinguished civility from politeness in chapter two, the two virtues share the same neighborhood, so to speak. I think Kingwell is right to find clues about civility in etiquette studies. I hope Kingwell receives a wide readership.

Kingwell errs, first, by misreading Alasdair MacIntrye on the conflict between traditions of practical rationality. This takes some explaining. The reader will remember MacIntyre's functional analysis of virtues in chapter three, an analysis found in *After Virtue*. Kingwell criticizes MacInyre for another, related idea which MacIntyre describes in a second book, *Whose Justice? Which Rationality?* Kingwell accuses MacIntyre of covertly assuming that some universal rationality will guarantee right outcomes when traditions of rationality conflict. Since MacIntyre emphatically argues that there is no universal rationality that can arbitrate between different worldviews, he is guilty of self-contradiction if Kingwell is right. I will argue, however, that Kingwell gives an uncharitable and inaccurate reading of MacIntyre.

More important to this book, Kingwell's misreading of MacIntyre grows out of a second mistake. Kingwell holds, throughout his book, to the traditional liberal priority of right over good, a notion that expresses itself in Audi's rules, examined in the last chapter, and in the work of many political philosophers. As this chapter progresses, I will explain what is meant by the priority of right over good, why we ought to question it, and to what degree we might want to retain it.

The General Structure of *A Civil Tongue*

Let's start with an overview of Mark Kingwell's book. Kingwell wants to advance a theory that he calls "justice as civility." To understand this idea, we must start with the tremendous diversity in contemporary democracies. For example, in the United States, which is the world's foremost example of a pluralist society, there are passionate adherents of many religions, convinced atheists, some agnostics, and lots of people for whom religion has little importance. Similar ranges of diversity can be found in relation to culture, art, and political ideology. In this great hodge-podge of beliefs, values, and practices, there is a great deal of overlap (on which advertisers and the entertainment media depend), but there is virtually no particular belief or value with universal approval. Philosophers' shorthand for this situation is to say that people in pluralist societies hold different, and incompatible "conceptions of the good."

How can we tell what justice is when we don't agree what the good life is? Take just one example: affirmative action. It doesn't take much attention to the arguments for and against affirmative action to realize that the disagreements go deeper than empirical questions like unemployment rates among urban African-Americans. All sides in affirmative action debates want justice, but they don't agree what justice is. Many philosophers have argued that in a pluralistic society justice cannot be defined in terms of any particular conception of the good, because there will always be people holding incompatible conceptions of the good, and for them "justice" as defined by the other groups would be injustice.

Kingwell counts himself among a number of philosophers who try to define justice dialogically. The basic idea is that proponents of different conceptions of the good engage each other in a political dialogue constrained by minimum rules of political speech. Whatever emerges from a properly structured dialogue is justice.

Kingwell calls his theory "justice as civility" because he thinks "civility" names the proper constraint, and the virtue that is the practice of proper constraint, of political speech. Describing this virtue, perhaps Kingwell should say "restraint" rather than "constraint." The virtuous citizen's speech is constrained, but it is self-constrained; she refrains from saying all she believes to be true.

Kingwell pays close attention to Bruce Ackerman, Alasdair MacIntyre, and Jurgen Habermas, each of whom contributes in different ways to discussion of dialogic notions of justice. He criticizes his sources, but thinks that they each add something useful to an emerging conception of properly constrained dialogue. In particular, Kingwell appreciates MacIntyre's insistence that an understanding of justice be rooted in a rich, full-bodied conception of the good. The thin, largely procedural theories of justice found traditionally among liberal thinkers (including Ackerman) fail, says Kingwell, to adequately address motivation and other connections between one's conception of the good and one's conception of justice.

In accepting what he reads as MacIntyre's call for a richly nuanced, contextualized understanding of justice, Kingwell turns to etiquette, both the books of instruction by purveyors of proper conduct and the few philosophers and sociologists who have given them scholarly attention. I will say little here about what Kingwell learns from the etiquette experts, except that he finds them helpfully illustrative of constrained speech—not saying all the true things one might say. Kingwell thinks that self-constraint in speech is a hallmark of civility. I think Kingwell's recourse to etiquette writers is right headed. Philosophers may be surprised by such resources, but they ought to be open to finding insight wherever they can.

How Kingwell misinterprets MacIntyre

Because Kingwell thinks justice in a pluralistic society emerges from civil dialogue, and since the hallmark of that dialogue is constrained speech, Kingwell thinks he must affirm a fairly common notion among liberal political theorists, the priority of right over good. The idea here is that in the political arena we cannot start with the multiple and incompatible conceptions of the good people have. As individuals we naturally seek to organize our lives around some rich conception of the good. But *as citizens*[2] we submit to a fairly minimal rule of right. Our political speech must be filtered by public rules for right speech. For instance, we should not appeal to the truth of our particular conception of the good as justification for public policy. We may propose some policy because it accords with our conception of the good (which may be religious or ideological in nature), but our political speech in support of that policy should appeal to reasons accessible to anyone in a pluralist society. Of course, a person may think that her conception of the good is pretty much true, but as a virtuous citizen, that is, one who practices civility, she will restrain herself from saying all she thinks is true. Kingwell and the philosophers he follows think that public dialogue constrained by these rules will produce an understanding of justice based on the right, not on any particular conception of the good.

It's easy to see how Robert Audi's principles of Christian citizenship that we examined in the last chapter fit into Kingwell's schema. As a Christian, Audi has a rich conception of the good. But he argues that as a citizen arguing in support of some public policy that restricts freedom, he should use only "secular reasons," reasons accessible to any person, not just those who share his particular religious or ideological commitments.

Alasdair MacIntyre's work presents a challenge to the priority of right over good and thus to Kingwell's structure for justice as civility. In *After Virtue* MacIntyre famously describes the enlightenment project in moral philosophy as doomed to failure. He criticizes liberal theories of justice as hopelessly thin, disconnected from robust moral traditions. MacIntyre's position is that *every* theory of justice is rooted in some conception of the good. Thus, modern theories of justice do not represent the minimal constraints of universal rationality, as their proponents imagine, but some particular conception of the good. To return to Audi's language, "secular reasons" for public policies simply don't exist, for all reasons given in support of any public policy reflect some conception of the good. According to MacIntyre, what we have in our contemporary situation is a contest between many conceptions of the good, each with its own understanding of justice, and enlightenment liberalism is just one of the contestants, not a neutral arbiter.

Kingwell appreciates MacIntyre's criticism of attempts to derive the rules of civil speech from the purely formal characteristics of rationality or rational speech. It is because he wants to heed MacIntyre's insistence on depth and background that Kingwell turns to etiquette experts to enrich his ideas about self-constraint in speech. But Kingwell cannot accept MacIntyre's position that all virtues—including justice—are grounded in a conception of the good.   Justice, he contends, will result from a rightly constrained dialogue. If we abandon the priority of right over good, he thinks, we have no protection against unrestrained political speech. After all, remember the Nazis. There are people who, in pursuit of power or some other value, will systematically and deliberately deceive, intimidate, blackmail, and destroy others with their political speech. How are we to think about the clash of political ideas? As simply a war between competing visions of the good? Why should we think, Kingwell asks, that the outcome of such a contest should be called justice?   The dialogic approach to justice requires that justice be the result of *rightly* constrained speech.

MacIntyre, in *Whose Justice? Which Rationality?*, described how the conversation between contending traditions of rational inquiry goes. Notice that here I am using MacIntyre-style language ("contending traditions of rational inquiry").   Reason, particularly practical reason, exists only in socially embodied traditions.   There cannot be, on MacIntyre's terms, a neutral rationality to stand as impartial arbiter between differing conceptions of the good life or differing theories of justice. Each tradition develops its own problems; as long as it solves its problems, or at least does not simultaneously encounter problems it cannot solve and some other tradition that can solve them, the tradition grows stronger.   Contact and conflict between rival traditions intensifies awareness of problems and possible solutions to them. It is possible that the adherents of some tradition of moral discourse/rational inquiry will convert to a superior tradition.   It is also possible, of course, that conflict between rival traditions may be prolonged over centuries, with no way of predicting the eventual outcome.

I think the previous paragragh is a fair précis of MacIntyre, and Kingwell would probably agree with it. But notice the crucial word. I said that adherents of some moral or rational tradition could convert to a "superior" tradition. It is just here that Kingwell accuses MacIntyre of inconsistency. If all rationality is traditional rationality, if there is no neutral rational judge between traditions, what does it mean to say that some tradition is superior to another? Either MacIntyre is endorsing some kind of natural selection of intellectual positions, Kingwell says, or he is covertly assuming some universal rational standard against which traditions of rationality can be measured. The first move is wrong, since it makes "superior tradition" simply mean "surviving tradition," which it doesn't. So Kingwell concludes that MacIntyre has covertly reintroduced the priority of right over good, in the form of an unspecified universal rationality by reference to which adherents of a tradition are able to recognize another tradition as superior to their own.[3]

I think there is a better way to read MacIntyre. On his account, it is the adherents of one moral and rational tradition that recognize the superiority of another. They don't step outside of themselves, in the sense of appealing to a universal standard, to make this judgment. They reason according to the standards of their own tradition, and in accord with those standards they find another tradition to be better.

In the contest between two traditions of inquiry, MacIntyre says, the better tradition will solve more (or more important) problems that are recognized as problems by both traditions. It will also explain how the deficient tradition fails to have the resources to solve the relevant problems. Now, Kingwell objects that MacIntyre is here covertly introducing universal standards of rationality (solving problems, explaining in the terms of one tradition how another cannot solve certain problems). But it is more charitable to interpret MacIntyre consistently with himself. MacIntyre insists that all standards of rationality grow out of some tradition or traditions. He is here referring to standards of rationality. He insists that all theories are judged as rational or not by the standards of some tradition. He is here presenting a theory. We should conclude that he offers his theory as a spokesman of some tradition.[4]   He is, I think, offering his interpretation of conversation between traditions both as a theory and as an illustration of that theory: how one tradition demonstrates its superiority to another. (The rival theory, of course, is the one MacIntyre tirelessly attacks: the liberal notion that we moderns stand outside traditions and thus have access to an absolute rational standard that we can apply to matters of practical reason.) His readers are invited to accept his theory, not on the basis of universal rational standards, but on the basis of their own standards.[5]   Of course, in accepting a new theory or tradition, a person will adopt a revised set of standards, but he does so on the basis of his old standards. At no point do we have to assume a super-traditional standard of rationality.[6]

How Kingwell errs about right and good

If I have suggested a better—that is, more charitable and accurate—reading of MacIntyre, Kingwell would probably object still that it offers little hope for managing the conflicts of political speech. With Habermas, Kingwell worries about the problems of deception and coercion.[7]   How likely is it, he might ask, that the adherents of one moral and rational tradition, on the basis of their own standards of rationality, will recognize another tradition as better? Do not some moral/rational traditions actively resist listening to the strengths of others? It isn't hard to find or imagine socially embodied traditions whose internal standards rule out the possibility of converting to a better tradition.   In political conversation they may attempt to systematically deceive their political opponents, using that deception to attain power with which to coerce their opponents.   Here we have political conversation, but it hardly seems productive of justice. We should judge such traditions as defective, but given MacIntyre's account of justice dialogue (at least, as I have reconstructed it), Kingwell worries that we can't. We would have to wait for such people to recognize the superiority of civil traditions. So Kingwell sticks with the priority of right over good. He thinks there may be something right in Habermas' idea that the very process of political conversation has an internal logic, so that there are minimal rational standards implicit in talk, but those standards will be so minimal that they won't give a good grounding for "just" talking (that is, talking that can produce justice).[8] Habermas' universal standards, if they exist, are truly universal, but too weak to ground real conversation. Kingwell pulls for a theory of dialogic justice based on "a weaker notion of universalism based on the shared commitments of forming and maintaining a society."[9] Kingwell's theory will be universal in the sense that it applies to everyone who accepts the goal of a civil society.

I don't see what Kingwell gains by this. He wants to maintain the priority of right over good, because he worries about participants in political dialogue who undermine civil society through deception or coercion. He sees that the priority of right over good depends on some transcontexual notion of rationality; he even accuses MacIntyre of covertly assuming some such notion. He thinks that Habermas' theory about the commitments implicit in conversation as such comes closest to supplying this universal standard, but he thinks, agreeing with many of Habermas' critics, that Habermas' theory is too idealized to do the job. In the end, then, he pulls for rules of right based on the commitments of certain people, those who are committed to civil society. This is not just a "weaker notion of universalism"; it's not universalism at all.

It is not true that all rational people share certain specifiable values, beliefs or practices simply because they are rational. Returning to MacIntyre's language, different traditions determine what is rational according to their own standards. So there are rational people who do not recognize the need for civility or other proper constraints on political speech.

Perhaps this is hard to believe. Rodney King said, "People, I just want to say, you know, can we all get along? . . . I mean, we're all stuck here for a while. Let's try to work it out."[10] King's practical reasoning is so clear, and the emotion of the message so right, that we may imagine that all people must acknowledge its force. Surely everyone sees that it is good and right and to our mutual advantage to try to "work it out." Surely anyone who fails to see this is just irrational.

Sorry. Some rational people do not see that it is good and right to try to work it out. Some rational people are committed to moral traditions that allow or esteem deception and force.

Kingwell's "weaker universalism" simply disenfranchises such people. The priority of right over good that he espouses will grow out of the real-world commitments of people who agree with Rodney King. Now, I think there is a sense in which such views ought to be disenfranchised. We ought to be committed to working things out together. But I think we should admit to ourselves that this is not universalism at all. The virtue of civility, to which Kingwell helpfully gives depth and substance by his use of etiquette studies and which I also prize, is a real virtue. But civility is recognized as a virtue in some moral traditions and not others. It is possible that in a pluralist culture such as ours a particular virtue may be very widely praised, but such trans-traditional agreement may be a historical accident, not a transcendental mark of truth. That is to say, truth is sought and defined within traditions of inquiry.

Recap

Mark Kingwell gets lots of things right in his book. Justice and our understanding of justice can grow out of civil dialogue. Our understanding of civility can be helpfully informed by studying etiquette.[11] Political theory and ethics in general need the rich treatment of virtues and traditions that Kingwell admires in MacIntyre.

But Kingwell gets some things wrong. He misinterprets MacIntyre, because MacIntyre does not appeal to universal rationality as Kingwell thinks. Kingwell's defense of the priority of right over good amounts to a virtual abandonment of the position; it would be better to admit that civility and other virtues grow out of some moral traditions and not others. In a postmodern time, when enlightenment modernism has been clearly identified as one tradition among many, such an admission may threaten the grounds for civility, which is why Kingwell clings to the priority of right over good.

We ought to pursue civility, and we may hope for better justice to emerge from civil discourse. We may find widespread agreement in this project, but this will only be because civility is recognized as a virtue by different traditions. *Why* it is a virtue is a matter for the next chapter.

Notes

[1] Kingwell, Mark. *A Civil Tongue: Justice, Dialogue, and the Politics of Pluralism.* (University Park, Pennsylvania: The Pennsylvania State University Press, 1995).

[2] Kingwell implies that true citizenship is restricted to those who practice civility, that is, constrain their speech. Obviously, this notion is not to be confused with legal citizenship of some state.

[3] "To the extent that MacIntyre wants a *normative* conversation between traditions, the rational force of 'the more adequate tradition' indicates a commitment to transcontextual reason." *A Civil Tongue*, p. 130.

[4] Since I approvingly use much of MacIntyre's work, both here and in chapter three, it is fair to ask whether I am not just a disciple. It is at just this point that MacIntyre's work is weakest. To read him sympathetically, we should read him as presenting himself as a participant in an intellectual tradition. But which one? Is he a Wittgensteinian? A Christian (more precisely, a Thomist)? MacIntrye never says, and his failure to do so shows that his picture of competing traditions is too simple to be taken at face value. The boundaries between traditions are blurry, and a real person may well inhabit more than

one. (Of course, MacInyre himself writes of "second first languages" in *After Virtue*—he is trying to say how discussion between rival traditions can happen. But many people are formed and live in the tension between traditions.)   For all his insistence on the complexity of moral discourse, MacIntyre's theory of intellectual traditions (if we call it that) is more theoretical outline than empirical description.

[5] MacIntyre makes this point fairly explicit.   *Whose Justice?   Which Rationality?*, p. 364: "When they have understood the beliefs of the alien tradition, they may find themselves compelled to recognize that within this other tradition it is possible to construct from the concepts and theories peculiar to it what they were unable to provide from their own conceptual and theoretical resources, a cogent and illuminating explanation—cogent and illuminating, that is, by their own standards— of why their own intellectual tradition had been unable to solve its problems or restore its coherence. The standards by which they judge this explanation to be cogent and illuminating will be the very same standards by which they have found their tradition wanting in the face of epistemological crisis."

[6] It might be argued that MacIntyre's perspectivism works *better* for those traditions of rationality that presume that there is some super-traditional standard of rationality (e.g. the mind of God), because in such traditions progressive theory choice can be seen as achieving closer and closer approximations of objective truth. But MacIntyre seems to have crafted his theory so that rational choice between traditions can be made without such assumptions.

[7] See Kingwell's example, *A Civil Tongue*, p. 127.

[8] *A Civil Tongue*, pp. 183-189.

[9] *A Civil Tongue*, p. 189.

[10] *Life Magazine*, June 1992.

[11] However, Kingwell's understanding that civility is primarily a constraint on speech is too narrow.   Civility moves one to treat one's political opponents well; undoubtedly that means we don't say all that we believe, but it means more than that.

Chapter Six:

A Basis for Civility

In this chapter I want to ask why anyone should be civil. To do so I will give a bit of civility's history, continue by predicting something of its future, and conclude by explaining what I believe to be civility's true ground, at least as I understand it.

Before I begin my history, though, we should note at least two senses in which we talk of a basis for a virtue. "Why should I be civil?" can mean, "Why is it a good thing, all things considered, for human beings to be civil?" and it can mean, "Why should a particular person (I), in a particular situation, be civil?" We could say that the first question asks for the metaphysical basis of the virtue while the second asks for the motivational basis of the virtue. Generally speaking, a satisfactory answer to the motivational question depends on a good answer to the first question, because if I, as a particular person, do not believe civility is a virtue for generic human beings, I will not likely believe it is a virtue in my own case. The motivational basis for civility depends on the metaphysical basis. Further, since we are often tempted to exempt ourselves from moral principles that we affirm in general (surely my situation qualifies as exceptional!), the metaphysical basis for civility needs to be of such a nature that a strong motivational basis can be built on it, strong enough to push me to pursue civility even when civility is costly.

Remember the definition of civility with which we are working: *a properly grounded character trait that moves an individual to treat political opponents well and/or to feel certain emotions toward political opponents, emotions that move an individual to treat political opponents well.*

Notice the qualification "properly grounded" in the definition. It is possible for someone to be motivated to treat his political opponents well for wrong reasons. Perhaps, like Aristotle's ignorant soldier, he does not understand the cost of virtue; he blithely assumes that everything will turn out fine. Just as we would not say that a soldier who fails to comprehend danger is truly brave, we would not say that a politician who could have no idea that treating his political opponents well might bring political defeat is truly civil. Or, like Aristotle's professional soldier, someone might exhibit a merely instrumental pseudo-virtue. If we treat political opponents well because we calculate that such behavior is the best way to win, we are not truly civil, just calculating.

True civility is the trait or traits of character that move one to treat one's political opponents well for the right reasons. Further on, I will suggest what I think those reasons should be. But first we should look at the reasons that have been traditionally given as grounds for civility.

A Modernist Virtue

In October 1555, Hugh Latimer was executed during the reign of England's "Bloody" Mary. He was burned at the stake with a fellow Protestant, Nicholas Ridley. As recorded in the martyrology, *Acts and Monuments*, by John Foxe, Latimer cried out when the fire was laid to the fuel: "Be of good comfort, Mr. Ridley, and play the man! We shall this day light such a candle, by God's grace, in England, as I trust never shall be put out."[1]

Latimer's courage when faced with death, and his good fortune to have his death recorded in a popular martyrology, made him into a hero/saint of the English Reformation. What generations of readers of Protestant history didn't read, however, was that some years before his own execution, Latimer presided over "a 'jolly muster,' as a traditional-minded friar, John Forest, was roasted alive over a fire made of a wooden statue of a saint hauled out of a pilgrimage church."[2]

Latimer's life and death is only one, though fairly gruesome, reminder that Christians have not always treated their political enemies well. Medieval and Reformation histories are replete with imprisonments, tortures, executions, and treacheries. Undoubtedly, many motivations and circumstances lie behind such behaviors. People acted out of greed, fear, superstition, hatred—the whole catalog of human sinfulness. But part of the reason for some of this incivility, particularly in a case like Latimer's, was philosophical.

All sides in reformation disputes assumed that there was such a thing as true doctrine. If someone rejected true doctrine, he earned God's judgment of eternal death, so if torture could bring about repentance, it was actually good for the offender. Further, the heretic was a public blasphemer who deserved death. Finally, innocent people might be corrupted if they listened to the heretic's ideas. Matters of truth, especially of religious truth, were regarded as having highest importance—literally infinite importance. These factors produced a *logic of intolerance.*

    1. Truth is of infinite value.
    2. We can identify the liars (people who deny/oppose the truth).
    3. Therefore, we have an over-riding duty to stop the liars.

In one form or another, this logic of intolerance shaped the thinking of Protestants and Catholics. Those with positions of influence or power, such as Queen Mary, or Latimer himself when he presided over Forest's death, felt they had a duty to do all they could to eliminate heresy.

We should remember all this, because the ideological contest between Protestants and Catholics formed much of the background to the emergence of modern philosophy. George Marsden likens the Protestant/Catholic conflict of the sixteenth and seventeenth centuries to the anti-Marxist/Marxist conflict of the twentieth; he calls it a "cold war." Both cold wars were protracted struggles, they were interrupted by "hot" wars, and they mixed nationalism with ideology.[3] Louis Dupré has argued recently that we should be wary of oversimplifying our accounts of the emergence of the modern worldview, and he is probably right; significant changes in European intellectual history going back to the thirteenth century are part of the story of the development of modernity.[4] Nevertheless, there is also merit in the traditional identification of the seventeenth and eighteenth centuries as the beginning of the modern era. Dupré describes the Enlightenment as a canonizing of options that had first been opened by the first phase of the passage to modernity.[5] One of those options, which the

Enlightenment canonized as a settled principle, was a turn from authority to rationality as ground for knowledge.

During the Catholic/Protestant cold war, both sides appealed to authority—of scripture or of church—to certify truth. Some early modern thinkers, from Descartes and Leibniz to Hume and Kant, appealed rather to reason. They saw this not only as intellectually better, since appeal to authority was akin to superstition while appeal to reason was akin to science, but also practically better, since religious appeals to authority could so easily support intolerance.

At this point we need to recount our history with care. Some people read the early modern period as a fairly simple tale of religious authoritarian intolerance versus skeptical rationalistic tolerance. Such a black/white story appeals to those who would see themselves as actors (Hume, Kant) or inheritors (21st century liberals) of the good side. According to such an interpretation, it was the Europe of 1648 and after, tired out by a hundred years of religious wars, that accepted a new world view. To be sure, the cold war continued, but it played a gradually decreasing role in international politics, and to an ever-increasing degree Europe's intellectuals looked to reason rather than authority to resolve philosophical debates.[6]

As Andrew R. Murphy argues, such a story is far too simple.[7] Most of the participants in seventeenth century debates over toleration in Britain and America were committed Christians, who offered distinctly religious rationales for toleration. The logic of intolerance could be opposed, on religious grounds, by a logic of tolerance:

> The arguments made by seventeenth-century tolerationists were almost exclusively Christian in nature: the true Christian displays humility and forbearance toward those with differing views; Jesus commanded preaching and not coercion; belief is beyond the control of the will and can only be brought about by persuasion; true belief requires the possibility of acting upon those beliefs without the fear of penal sanctions.[8]

Toleration is not the same thing as civility, but the two virtues must be related. What Murphy says about the rise of toleration would probably be true, *mutatis mutandis*, about civility. In the early modern era, the idea that we ought to treat our political opponents with respect and dignity gained support, not just from Enlightenment philosophy, but also from theological arguments. Below, in "Solid Ground for Civility," I will suggest what such theological arguments might be like.

However, for liberals of the nineteenth and twentieth centuries, it is rationalistic, anti-authoritarian philosophy, not theological arguments, that best grounds civility. Such liberals look back to philosophers like Hume, and especially Kant, not to a religious authority, for a worldview in which political enemies are treasured. For Kant, the key fact about any person, and thus any political opponent, is that person's status as a rational being. If reasonable people can differ, and if a person's dignity is founded on his or her reason, then even people who disagree with each other ought to be able to respect and tolerate each other. On this reading of history, it is not a remarkable coincidence that while Kant was explaining that the categorical imperative, which was the product of reason alone, required that we treat all people as ends and not merely means, Thomas Jefferson and other American reformers were enshrining religious freedom and toleration as fundamental principles of government. It was a fundamental assumption of the Enlightenment, which Kant only made more explicit than most of his contemporaries, that Reason was the same for all people. Liberals who read seventeenth century history as the triumph of rationalism over authority will ground civility in rationalism. Universal rationality is the Enlightenment modernist basis for civility.

Postmodern Prospects for Civility

We live, as the culture watchers constantly din into our ears, in a post-modern world. If Dupré is right, in one sense this is simply not true. Our culture is still working out the implications of the breakup of the ancient and medieval worldviews; in that sense we are still moderns. What the culture watchers have right is that we no longer accept some of the principles of the Enlightenment.

To illustrate: The modernist (whether of the fourteenth century, the eighteenth century or the twentieth century) believes that the *now* is a significantly new thing.[9] All modernists believe that the contingencies of time produce *fundamental* reshapings of knowledge and reality. (Ancient and medieval world views denied that true knowledge or reality could undergo fundamental change.) Some modernists, Enlightenment modernists, believed that changes over time exhibited progress. Some contemporary modernists, who call themselves post-modernists because they define modernism by the Enlightenment, have come to disbelieve in progress. They worry: If the human race is not progressing morally, is it really good that we are gaining more technological power? So, while all modernists (in Dupré's sense) believe that time has produced basic change, some of them have given up thinking that change is progress.

Something significant happens when our contemporaries reject principles of the Enlightenment, even if "post-modernism" may be an inappropriate description of that rejection. Now, one of the most widely proclaimed post-modernist (or anti-Enlightenment) assumptions is the rejection of universal rationality. The standards of reason, especially the standards of practical reason, which Enlightenment philosophers like Kant assumed to be universal, are labeled partial and parochial by post-modernists. Some people, who accept certain assumptions about individualism, objectivism, and self-interested rationality—that is, people with Enlightenment worldviews—will approach problems of practical reason in ways that Kant or Hume or Hobbes would recognize as rational. But other people do not think that way. So "rationality" means different things to different peoples, say the post-modernists.

This post-modern rejection of universal reason is surely right. Alasdair MacIntyre, in *Whose Justice? Which Rationality?*, persuades me that even in the West we have several different traditions of practical reason competing for our allegiance.[10]   Autonomous reason, a capitalized "Reason" that stands alone independent of historically conditioned reasoners, does not exist unless in the mind of God.

So the Enlightenment assumption of universal rationality is undermined. At the least, Enlightenment modernists need to give some story justifying their belief in universal rationality. Post-modernists find they no longer believe in it. What happens to civility in these conditions? What happens to the motivational basis for civility if a widely believed metaphysical basis for civility ceases to be believed?

For an Enlightenment modernist, a political opponent can be assumed to be a reasonable person. The political opponent can be appealed to on grounds of good evidence or clear reasoning. The political opponent, a reasonable person, is worthy of respect, even if disagreements persist between competing parties. The implications of Kant's categorical imperative are quite clear: We can work to defeat our political opponents—in a sense, they are obstacles to be overcome, means to our ends—but we may never treat political opponents as *merely* obstacles. We must always treat them as ends in themselves. Even further, since our worst political opponents are rational seekers of truth, they are actually our allies. Through vigorous debate, seekers pursue the truth together.

But post-modernists need not believe this. The post-modernist does not assume that all people are "reasonable." Rather, some people are reasonable in one way, while others are reasonable in another way, and still others are reasonable in still other ways—and the various kinds of rationality may be incommensurable and irreconcilable. There is no way to appeal to all political enemies on the grounds of evidence (they may not see the evidence as relevant) or good reasons (they may reject the assumptions behind the reasons). Therefore there is no compelling need to treat political enemies with respect. After all, some political enemies are most easily dealt with summarily: we see them just as obstacles. There is no independent standard of rationality that would require us to treat them as more than obstacles.

Some post-modernists, like Richard Rorty, still urge civility and other liberal values. But he does not urge this on the basis of some truth about the universe or ourselves. Rather, this is just the way liberal people happen to feel.[11]

I suspect that we shall soon hear from post-modern voices that do not urge civility. Like Nietzsche, they will call us to a bracing acceptance of our "thisness": "I am this, and I want that. My political enemy is that which stands between me and the fulfillment of my desire." From a subjectivist point of view, the enemy is and can be nothing more than an obstacle. And there is no objective point of view (objectivity is another Enlightenment concept deconstructed by post-modernists) to correct the subjectivist's point of view.

In short, I predict dark days ahead for civility. To the degree that civility inhabits our political culture, civility is largely the gift of Enlightenment assumptions that many people in our culture no longer make. Those who feel like it, or whose historically contingent way of exercising practical reason recommends it, will continue to treat their political opponents well and train themselves in the virtues that motivate such behavior. But as people come to recognize their feelings in this regard and the ways they have learned to think about this matter as pure historical accidents, they will have little defense against the temptations of incivility.

Solid Ground for Civility

All of this suggests an historical irony, at least for liberals who read the early modern period in the simple, good-skeptical-rationalist versus bad-authoritarian-religionist, way that many do. Though, on that account, we moderns have learned to regard civility as a virtue through the influence of Enlightenment modernism, it is Christian doctrine, not Enlightenment philosophy, which provides a sufficient foundation for civility.

This may seem surprising. After all, it is religious beliefs, for instance, the Christian assumption that true doctrine had great importance, that lay behind a logic of intolerance. "Since the truth is of infinite value, the heretic must be made to see that it is the truth." Right?

Wrong. The assumption that truth exists is not the problem. We need further assumptions to make the logic of intolerance work. First, we need to think, not only that truth is valuable, but also that we have the right formulation of the truth. Second, we must assume that we have access to the right formulation of the truth independent of the thought of those who disagree with us. Third, we must believe that the truth is itself compatible with intolerance. A "fallibilist" rejects the first two of these assumptions; that is, a fallibilist will always keep alive in her mind the possibility that she is wrong, and she will believe that opposing views may be useful—perhaps necessary—in the pursuit of truth. Some philosophers have suggested that fallibilism is, or is part of, the cure for intolerance.[12]   In the next chapter, I will say more about a fallibilist process of truth seeking. For the present, however, I want to take issue with the third assumption just mentioned.

Many parties to Reformation disputes, and many political groups in the generations since, have assumed that truth is compatible with the forcible suppression of error. They have thought that truth is so important that error must be suppressed. But what if the content of truth was itself incompatible with incivility? If that were the case, it would be possible for a person to believe truth with absolute certainty, even believe that opposing views are useless in the pursuit of truth, and still have good reasons for being civil.[13] Or—as Murphy points out—if it is crucial that persons come to see the truth for themselves, as the Protestant emphasis on faith implies, the religious believer could again hold his belief with absolute certainty and still have good reasons for civility.

My belief is that truth is incompatible with intolerance or incivility. Proper grounds for civility may be found in fallibilism, but also in the truth itself. I do not have to be uncertain of the doctrines I espouse to listen attentively to those who disagree with me; rather, the content of those doctrines may require it.

What truth or doctrines could I be referring to? Just this, the heart of Christianity: Jesus Christ died for sinners, that is, for his enemies.

Christian dogma teaches us that we, who made ourselves God's enemies, are the objects of his love. His love overcame that enmity and made us his friends, through the cross. Jesus' words, expressed on the cross about the particular soldiers who crucified him, express his attitude toward all his enemies: "Father, forgive them, for they don't know what they're doing." (Luke 23:34)

Christian truth requires civility in at least three ways. 1. Because God, in Christ, loved his enemies, Christians have no option but to try to love their enemies. Christ is our example. 2. Further, Jesus explicitly told his followers to love their enemies. Christ is our lawgiver. 3. Further still, as the light of the world, Jesus is the light in every person. We should look for the light of Christ in everyone, including our enemies. Christ is our *logos* of civility.[14]

It should be noted that this Christian basis for civility is distinctly non-modern. Christians think and reason as inheritors of a tradition that recognizes authority. A Christian tradition of practical reason unapologetically refers to the truth and to attempts to ascertain the truth.[15] Such a tradition competes with other traditions, in MacIntyre's analysis, by showing itself able to solve problems of practical reason which they can't (and by explaining why they can't). Liberals in a postmodern culture who cherish civility may, according to their own lights, discover that such a Christian tradition of practical reason that grounds civility is superior to a postmodern mindset that undermines it.

Part of the irony, of course, is that though Christians have always had perfectly good reasons to treat their enemies well, they often failed to do so. It's likely that some Christians in the later modern period (the nineteenth and twentieth centuries) learned more civility from Enlightenment philosophers than from the toleration arguments of their seventeenth century forbears. This was not just because Christians failed to live up to their understanding of the gospel, but also because they partly failed to understand the gospel.

If my earlier prediction comes true, we will hear Nietzsche-like post-modern voices that forthrightly reject civility. I hope my prediction does not come true; it would be better to live in a culture that honors civility than to be an accurate forecaster. But even if some around us find that they no longer have reasons to be civil, Christians should not be deterred from training themselves in this virtue. We want to be like Christ; we want to obey his commands; and we want to recognize Christ in all people, including our political opponents.[16]

Notes

[1] "A Tale of Two Martyrs," *Christian History* (Vol. XIV, No. 4), pp. 18-19.

[2] Martin, Dennis. "Catholic Counterpoint: What was it like to be on the losing side of England's Reformation?" *Christian History* (Vol. XIV, No. 4), p. 30.

[3] See George Marsden, *Religion and American Culture* (Fort Worth, Texas: Harcourt Brace College Publishers, 1990), pp. 12-13.

[4] See Louis Dupre', *Passage to Modernity.* (New Haven, Connecticut: Yale University Press, 1993). To oversimplify, Dupre''s thesis is that the Enlightenment, which is usually thought of as the beginning of the modern era, was the second of two important revolutions in thought that transformed the medieval world into the modern world. His book charts the first, largely thirteenth century, revolution.

[5] Dupre', p. 253.

[6] It's easy to overstate and oversimplify. Medieval philosophers and theologians did not denigrate reason. But, like Aquinas, they sought to bring their theorizing under the authority of church, creed, and scripture. I take it that one mark of a modern philosopher is that he or she will not submit the products of philosophical investigation to external authority.

[7] Andrew R. Murphy. *Conscience and Community.* (University Park, Pennsylvania: The Pennsylvania State University Press, 2001). For an initial exposition of "three myths" about religious toleration in the early modern period, see pp. 11-16.

[8] Murphy, p. 13.

[9] See Dupre', p. 145.

[10] Alasdair MacIntyre, *Whose Justice? Which Rationality?* (Notre Dame, Indiana: University of Notre Dame Press, 1988). See pp. 1-11 for an initial statement of his position, which is argued at length throughout the book. See also the discussion of MacIntyre in chapter five of this book.

[11] Richard Rorty, *Contingency, Irony, and Solidarity* (Cambridge: Cambridge University Press, 1989). See, for instance, p. 189: " . . . a belief can still regulate action, can still be thought worth dying for, among people who are quite aware that this belief is caused by nothing deeper than contingent historical circumstance." And pp. 197-98: "There is no *neutral*, noncircular way to defend the liberal's claim that cruelty is the worst thing we do, any more than there is a neutral way to back up Nietzsche's assertion that this claim expressed a resentful, slavish attitude . . . . We cannot look back behind the processes of socialization which convinced us twentieth-century liberals of the validity of this claim and appeal to something which is more 'real' or less ephemeral than the historical contingencies which brought those processes into existence. *We* have to start where *we* are . . ."

[12] See Philip L. Quinn, "Political Liberalisms and Their Exclusions of the Religious," the Presidential Address delivered at the 93rd Annual Central Division Meeting of the American Philosophical Association, in *Proceedings and Addresses of the American Philosophical Association* (Vol. 69, No. 2), p.

47. Quinn agrees with other writers who think that fallibilism ought not to be a requirement of discourse in the public square, since such a requirement would exclude certain religious traditions, which explicitly reject fallibilism, from joining in political debate.

It might help to remember the form of fallibilism of the dissenting puritans in the Westminster Assembly, who helped move English society from the religious wars of the sixteenth century to the *Act of Toleration* in 1689. Although the Dissenters did not carry the day during the Westminster Assembly, they argued that differences of opinion among Christians were due to the weakness of human apprehension of the truth, and that differences of opinion could lead to fuller apprehension of the truth. Thus, the Dissenters' position anticipated that of fallibilists (and the procedure described in the next chapter). See Rex Koivisto, *One Lord, One Faith: A Theology for Cross-Denominational Renewal* (Wheaton, Illinois: Victor Books/SP Publications, Inc. 1993), pp. 98-101.

[13] Since I do not believe opposing views are useless in the pursuit of truth, I am clearly not describing my own position. Perhaps I am describing only a theoretical possibility. But it is an important one; too often we assume that religious beliefs intensely held must produce intolerance.

[14] Readers might compare this idea—that Christ is the *logos* of our civility—to Arthur Roberts' paper, "Good and Evil in a World Threatened by Nuclear Omnicide: A Proposed Epistemological Paradigm." The paradigm Roberts proposes posits rational, sensory, and intuitive modes of apprehending truth, modes which different individuals combine in varying ways. Such a model reinforces for us the need to listen to others. Other people, even political opponents, can teach us something of the *logos*, the center toward which we must move if we want to progress morally, intellectually, or esthetically.

[15] Some people might find it an advantage of such a tradition that it has the resources to talk about truth and the pursuit of truth, as compared to some worldviews that exclude such concepts.

[16] A version of this chapter appeared as "A Basis for Civility," in *Truth's Bright Embrace: Essays and Poems in Honor of Arthur O. Roberts*, eds. Paul Anderson and Howard Macy. (Newberg, Oregon: George Fox University Press, 1996), pp. 335-343. I owe thanks to Paul Anderson for helpful comments on drafts of that paper.

Chapter Seven:

Civility and Civil Process

This chapter comes at civility from a different perspective than the last three. We have been thinking about civility philosophically, trying to relate civility to ethical theory, theology, and political philosophy. But some readers of the first six chapters will want real world applications of our philosophizing. That is, if civility is a virtue for disagreements and controversies, what does it look like in practice? In chapter one, I said that there is a way to conduct our controversies civilly. What is it?

Much of the content of this chapter comes from three sources: Roger Fisher and William Ury's *Getting to Yes*, Mark Juergensmeyer's *Fighting Fair*, and Marvin T. Brown's *Working Ethics*. These are by no means the only authors presenting models for what we may call "civil process" in conflict resolution or business management literature, but they are representative. Though they use varying terminology, these authors share certain important ideas that outline civil process.

Fisher and Ury, Juergensmeyer, and Brown do not address the virtue of civility directly in terms of moral theory. They are interested in practical "how to" questions: how to negotiate a wise agreement, how to "fight" an opponent on Gandhian principles, how to make ethical business decisions. Along the way, they necessarily talk about attitudes and behaviors that help produce success in the civil process they seek to describe. In that sense, they do talk about civility, and their comments are insightful. After distilling an outline of civil process from a comparison of my three sources, I will try to say what civil process can teach us about civility.

Fisher and Ury: *Getting to Yes*

Arising out of the Harvard Negotiation Project, *Getting to Yes*[1] is a widely translated, best-selling guide to "negotiating agreement without giving in." The authors have in mind all sorts of negotiation situations: nations trying to find peace (or prevent war), divorcing spouses dividing property, management and labor seeking a new contract, buyer and seller settling on a price, corporations contemplating merger, and so on. Thus, the scope of "negotiation" in *Getting to Yes* is as broad as politics as I defined it in chapter two, the art or science of making group decisions.

Fisher and Ury start by noting that most people tend to engage in "positional" negotiation. That is, one person or side states a position and gives reasons why it should be adopted. The other side states a contrary position. In positional negotiation the two (or more) sides usually proceed to fight for their views in a number of ways: with reasons or threats, delays, promises, compromises, etc. Participants choose between "soft" or "hard" positional strategies[2], and the negotiation ends in one of a few predictable ways: surrender by one side or the other, a compromise (split the difference), or a breakdown in negotiation. In positional bargaining, the only sure way to reach agreement is to give in, and Fisher and Ury urge their readers to find a better way.

Fisher and Ury argue that positional negotiation should be rejected, because it is inefficient, it endangers relationships, and it produces "unwise" agreements. "A wise agreement can be defined as one which meets the legitimate interests of each side to the extent possible, resolves conflicting interests fairly, is durable, and takes community interests into account."[3] In contrast to positional negotiation, Fisher and Ury offer "principled" negotiation, or "negotiation on the merits," which they reduce to four slogans:

1. Separate the people from the problem.
2. Focus on interests, not positions.
3. Invent options for mutual gain.

4. Insist on using objective criteria.[4]

Fisher and Ury devote a chapter to each of these instructions, and they illustrate their principles with plenty of examples. Here, a summary will suffice.

First, a negotiator needs to recognize that all negotiation processes have two components, the matter to be decided and the relationship between the people involved.[5] Fisher and Ury urge their readers to deal directly with relationship issues and to disentangle the human relationships in a negotiation from the substance of the negotiation. The idea is not that relationship issues are somehow less important than "substantive problems," only that each needs separate attention. Too often, negotiations go awry because criticisms of someone's position are heard as criticisms of that person. A principled negotiator strives to maintain good relationships between the persons in the negotiation, separating the people from the problem.

Second, a negotiator should not worry too much about the stated, conflicting positions of the various sides (including her own). Instead, she should ask *why* each side takes the position it does. That is, what are the underlying "interests" which each participant is trying to serve through his stated position?[6] Almost certainly, a person's interests can be served by many possible solutions, not just the one in his stated position. The positions that people bring to negotiations are usually incompatible, but the interests behind those positions often aren't. A major advantage of the first step (separate people from the problem) appears here, if people on both sides can come to see themselves as partners, working together to solve a common problem rather than as win-lose enemies.[7] The problem they share is, of course, finding a solution that serves the interests (not the positions) of both sides.

Third, a negotiator should invent options. Fisher and Ury urge their readers to abandon certain obstacles to inventiveness: premature criticism of ideas; thinking that there is a single, perfect solution to be found; assuming a "fixed pie"—that the gains of one side must come from the losses of someone else; and believing that the other side should be solely responsible to look out for its own interests.[8] Then, working either alone or with the other side, negotiators should brainstorm, writing down idea after idea, letting one proposal suggest another, without subjecting them to criticism. Only after many ideas have been collected should the negotiators decide which, if any, will contribute to a solution to their problem.

Fourth, negotiators should insist that any agreement be based on objective criteria.[9] Fisher and Ury warn that positional bargaining often reduces to a contest of wills; whichever side is strongest or most stubborn wins in the end, which is no way to ensure wise decisions. Instead, negotiators should insist that a solution be based on "fair standards." There are many possible sources of fair standards: tradition, market value, expert opinion, what a court would decide, etc. The key feature of all these possible fair standards is that they are independent of each side's will.[10] A principled negotiator is committed to neither his own criteria nor his initial position; he is open to any solution which serves the interests of all the parties and which is based on objective criteria.

Fisher and Ury do not claim that principled negotiation always works. One side in a negotiation may want to negotiate on the merits, but run into someone who persistently refuses. Sometimes parties in negotiations are unwilling to tie proposed solutions to objective criteria, or they are not willing to allow that the interests of the other side matter. Fisher and Ury urge negotiators to consider and improve their "BATNA"—their best alternative to a negotiated agreement.[11] Sometimes a negotiator is better off walking away from a negotiation with no agreement than an agreement reached by yielding in a positional negotiation. She should consider before negotiations begin what her best alternative to an agreement would be.

However, a principled negotiator can succeed more often than one might expect. Fisher and Ury recommend "negotiation jujitsu" be tried on recalcitrant opponents who cling to positional bargaining.[12] When an opponent pushes, the principled negotiator does not push back. Instead, she redirects or reframes the opponent's moves. When an opponent presents a take it or leave it position, the principled negotiator assumes that this is instead one option among many. She assumes that the opponent has offered it as an attempt to serve everyone's interests and asks how the proposal achieves that purpose. The principled negotiator does not defend her own proposals, but asks for criticism and advice, in order to produce more options. When the opponent attacks her personally, she recasts the attack as an attempt to solve the problem. Often, say Fisher and Ury, "you can change the game simply by starting to play a new one."[13]

That is the key idea: how we negotiate is just as important as any solution the negotiation produces. The negotiator should insist on playing a principled game. If you play the right game, you don't have to lose.

Mark Juergensmeyer: *Fighting Fair*

Previously published as *Fighting with Gandhi*, Mark Juergensmeyer's book explains how Mahatma Gandhi's principles of *satyagraha* constitute a "non-violent strategy for resolving everyday conflicts."[14] Juergensmeyer thinks (and certainly Gandhi did too) that *satyagraha* applies to all sorts of conflicts, from very large (India's fight for independence, Gandhi's campaign for rights for untouchables) to personal and intimate. Like Fisher and Ury, the scope of Juergenmeyer's work fits the broad definition of politics of chapter two.

Satyagraha means, "grasping onto principles" or "truth force."[15] Gandhi was a pacifist, committed to non-violence, yet he was deeply engaged in political fights throughout his adult life. Juergensmeyer presents Gandhi's ideas as guidance for fighters.

> The approach to fighting we are about to encounter is just that: it is based on the premise that effective fighting does not require you to abandon your humanity, even if you are faced with the most recalcitrant and ferocious opponent. You can be sensible and generous in your fighting, and you can win.[16]

How? The "steps in a fair fight":

1. Recognize truthful and untruthful elements in each side.
2. Put the truthful elements together.
3. Form a new side and adopt it while struggling with your opponent.
4. Revise the new position even as the fight continues.
5. End the struggle when both sides agree to occupy the same side.[17]

It will help to notice both similarities and differences between the Gandhian fair fight and Fisher and Ury's principled negotiation.

First, both approaches are explicitly aimed at situations of conflict and opposition. They see conflict as normal, even something to be welcomed, certainly not something to be avoided.

Second, the Gandhian fighter and the principled negotiator look for something deeper or behind the initial position of each side. Fisher and Ury call this something the "interests" of the bargainers; Gandhi calls it the truthful elements of each side. Both approaches assume that there is something right in almost every position. The opponent's proposal may sound outrageous (it may actually be outrageous), yet it harbors a legitimate interest of a real person; it expresses some truth that the opponent knows. The principled negotiator and the Gandhian fighter want to make common cause with the interests/truth that the opponent brings to the situation.

Third, both procedures emphasize creativity. The Gandhian fighter takes the truthful elements of both sides and creates a new side—and then adopts it. The principled negotiator invents lots of options before criticizing them. Both are willing to abandon their previous positions on outcomes. They are always willing to accept a new solution, but only if the new solution is more truthful or better serves peoples' interests.

Fourth, both approaches acknowledge the uncooperativeness of some opponents. Fisher and Ury believe that principled negotiation is contagious; many opponents will be drawn into the challenge of finding creative solutions to a mutual problem.[18] Similarly, Gandhi thought *satyagraha* would draw in many opponents. But sometimes there will be stubborn opponents who do not want to negotiate on the merits or participate in a truth seeking process. The Gandhian fighter and the principled negotiator are not surprised by such resistance, but they are not deflected by it either. In Fisher and Ury's term, they use "negotiation jujitsu"; they continue to play a new game and reinterpret the opponent's moves as attempts to help the new game.

Gandhi is more emphatic than Fisher and Ury on this point. The Harvard scholars think that "negotiation jujitsu" will often succeed in bringing the stubborn opponent into principled negotiation—but not always. Sometimes, they say, a negotiator needs to walk away from a hopeless negotiation. For Gandhi, *satyagraha* represented a whole philosophy of life, not just a way of fighting political opponents. How can one abandon "grasping onto principles"? Ideally, the Gandhian fighter would never give up the search for a truthful solution. Sometimes the Gandhian fighter might discover deficiencies in himself and thus break off a fight for a time of spiritual reflection and renewal[19], but he would always come back to the fight. (Remember, the goal of a Gandhian fight is to find a solution based on truth.)

Gandhi's method of fighting is explicitly and crucially nonviolent.[20] *Ahimsa* ("nonviolence") meant, for Gandhi, a lack even of desire for violence or coercion. Gandhi taught that a fighter could be forceful without being coercive; that is, he would always leave room for the opponent to choose. Coercion happens when someone is forced to act against his will.[21] Fisher and Ury do not go nearly this far. For them, principled negotiation is a practical method, not a spiritual path.

Marvin Brown: *Working Ethics*

Marvin Brown gives advice for people who seek to make better decisions—morally better decisions—in organizational settings.[22] He does not speak directly to conflict situations, nor does he have in mind state politics or family politics, so his focus is narrower than the notion of politics we have been using. But Brown would not be surprised if the civil process for working groups he describes is similar to civil process in other situations.

There are five resources for the decision making process, which Brown calls "discovering the right decision": proposals, observations, value judgments, basic assumptions, and opposing views.[23] Already we see similarities between Brown's approach and that of Fisher and Ury or Gandhi. Moral decision making is a *process* that *discovers*; it is not a defense of what we already know. In that process, opposing views are a resource, not an obstacle.

We start, Brown says, with the policy proposals that people make. Then ask, "Why?"

> If you ask why someone believes we should adopt a certain policy, she or he will inevitably point to observations, value judgments, or assumptions that support the conclusion. By examining these supports, we can discover the grounds on which the proposal is based and we can then better assess its strengths and weaknesses.[24]

Observations are factual claims that the working group can verify empirically. Suppose the policy proposal is that the company ought to provide daycare for its employees. Someone asks, "Why?" An initial answer might be, "Because 15% of our workers have preschool children." By itself, this answer isn't enough, but it's helpful. Brown wants his readers to see factual information as a resource for morally better decisions. To justify moral decisions, facts have to be tied to values. The justification for the day care proposal might continue, "And we value the well-being of our employees' children."

Often, people in working groups will agree about value judgments and still disagree about the policy proposals based on them. The group's members make different assumptions about the way the world works. So the justification for the day care proposal might add, "And we believe day care programs are cost effective ways of promoting the well-being of our employees' children."

Disagreement in the working group can occur at any point, and Brown admits that disagreements over assumptions may be the most difficult to resolve.[25]   But the process of distinguishing proposals, observations, value judgments, and assumptions allows the group to identify what it needs to work on to reach clearness. "Agreement, of course, is never guaranteed in ethical reflection, but finding out why people disagree can surely help us develop a better course of action."[26]

Even when we have agreed on a course of action, opposing views can help supply what Brown calls an "unless."[27]   We recognize that our decision is based on certain assumptions we have made about the way the world works. We don't have to ignore the strengths of opposing views; we can use them to build in qualifications to our plan. For example, "The company will provide day care for its employees, *unless* participation rates fall below a certain level (which may indicate that child care is not advancing the well-being of children) or costs rise past a certain point (which may indicate that child care is not cost effective)."

Brown's general scheme of a moral decision, then, is this: We will do x, because we observe a, b, and c; and because we value e, f, and g, and we believe h, i, and j; unless m, n, or o occur.[28]

Brown knows that some of his readers can scarcely imagine such a process succeeding in the work groups with which they are familiar. So he devotes a chapter to "creating conditions for ethical reflection."[29] These conditions are:

*Power—each member of the group should believe that his contribution to group process matters, and the group as a whole should believe that its final decision would be implemented;

*Trust—group members should be confident that the others in the group would not manipulate them by appeals to status or emotion;

*Inclusion—to the extent possible, the group includes all the parties who will be affected by the decision, and group members try to take into account the interests of absent parties;

*Role Flexibility—group members should occasionally take on others' positions, to state the needs and interests of the other as if they were the other; and

*Inquiry—group members should seek to understand before making decisions or criticizing possible options.

Brown acknowledges that some working groups have little of these conditions for ethical reflection. Individuals may feel trapped in working situations where cynicism, selfishness, and evil are the rule. Change comes as individuals, especially leaders, try to create the conditions of ethical reflection in their work groups. As in so many things, practice makes better.

Civil Process

Even with such a short survey of only three sources in a burgeoning literature[30], we can identify advices for civil process. First, concentrate on the process as much as on outcomes. All three sources emphasize that the way we go about deciding a political issue is as important as the decision.

Second, look for the interests, truths, or values that lie behind policy positions. In MBA ethics classes, I have sometimes used the ambiguous phrase, "Look for the stuff behind the stuff." People come into politics (call it negotiation, fighting, or group decision making) with "stuff": claims, proposals, complaints, etc. A civil process will ask *why*—from their point of view, what truth or need or feeling is expressed in the initial statement? This "stuff" (interests, truths, needs)—which comes out later, the "stuff behind the stuff"—will be the ingredients for a solution.

Third, sort things out. Fisher and Ury tell us to separate people from positions, and Brown says to separate observations from value judgments and assumptions. A civil process doesn't have to operate by set procedural rules, but it often helps to focus on one thing at a time.

Fourth, seek to make common cause. A civil process is an open invitation to all concerned to join in a truth-seeking, problem solving process. All the participants are on the same side (at least, they can be, if they are willing), trying to find a creative solution to a problem shared by all.

Fifth, be creative. Assume that the possible range of solutions is bigger than anyone has yet thought. Persistently seek a solution that meets the legitimate needs of everyone concerned. Don't accept quick compromises or one-sided solutions—better solutions take more work to discover, but they provide more stable results.

Civil Process and Civility

I hope the little I've said in this chapter gives the reader a picture of what civil process can be like. A full discussion of civil process would be a book in itself, taking us away from our topic, the virtue of civility.

Readers who want more detail about civil process would do well to read Fisher and Ury, Juergensmeyer or Brown.

What can civil process teach us about civility? As I have said, there is a cost to civility. If we treat our political opponents well, they may defeat us. If we consider only the cost of civility, we might be tempted to think of civility as an impossible ideal. Brown, Juergensmeyer, and Fisher and Ury counter this temptation. They promise that civil process can work—perhaps not always, but often. (Gandhi would promise more; *satyagraha* always "works" in the sense of being the right way to live.) So the first thing civil process teaches about civility is this: civility can be the partner of hope. Persons who engage in civil process are entitled to a reasonable expectation of success. And there is a second sense in which civil process engenders hope. Civil process is something that can be practiced, and it involves skills that can be learned, so all three sources encourage us to believe that we can get better. Our habits up to now may have been those of positional negotiators, or violent fighters, or cynical workers—but we can change. Civility is partner to hope.

Second, civil process involves discovery. It relieves us of the burden of having to have a correct or acceptable solution to a political problem at the beginning of the process. Principled negotiators or Gandhian fighters are happy to admit that they do not have the right solution; they enter civil process in order to find a right solution. So civility is a partner to learning and curiosity.[31]

Third, civil process involves listening to contrary views. Brown's conditions of "power" and "inquiry" describe a kind of confidence a civil person places in the political opponent. The political opponent knows her interests, her truth, better than we do. We can count on her to care about those interests, that truth. Persons who engage in civil process depend on the political opponent to advance the search for truth-based solutions by bringing these resources to the process. So civility is partner to confidence in the opponent.

Hope, curiosity, and confidence in the opponent: I don't suggest these are all that civil process can teach us about civility. In keeping with my sources, though, I remind the reader that civil process is a matter of praxis. We will learn what it has to teach about civility as we actually engage in civil process.

Notes

[1] Roger Fisher, William Ury, and Bruce Patton, *Getting to Yes: Negotiating Agreement Without Giving In,* 2nd. ed., New York: Penguin Books, 1991.

[2] Fisher, Ury, and Patton, p. 9.

[3] Fisher, Ury, and Patton, p. 4. Compare this description of a wise agreement with the discussion of better decisions, the *telos* of politics, in chapter 3 (pp. 29-30).

[4] Fisher, Ury, and Patton, pp.11-13.

[5] Fisher, Ury, and Patton, pp. 18-22.

[6] Fisher, Ury, and Patton, pp. 40-43.

[7] Fisher, Ury, and Patton, p. 37.

[8] Fisher, Ury, and Patton, pp. 57-59.

[9] Fisher, Ury, and Patton, pp. 81-84.

[10] Fisher, Ury, and Patton, p. 85.

[11] Fisher, Ury, and Patton, pp. 99-103.

[12] Fisher, Ury, and Patton, pp. 107-12.

[13] Fisher, Ury, and Patton, p. 107 and p. 116.

[14] Mark Juergensmeyer, *Fighting Fair: A Non-Violent Strategy for Resolving Everyday Conflicts*. New York: Harper and Row, 1986.

[15] Juergensmeyer, p. 3.

[16] Juergensmeyer, p. vii.

[17] Juergensmeyer, p. 21.

[18] Fisher, Ury, and Patton, p. 107.

[19] As Gandhi sometimes did. See Juergensmeyer, pp. 61-62.

[20] Juergensmeyer, p. 27.

[21] Juergensmeyer. p. 29. See also the discussion of coercion in chapter eight.

[22] Marvin T. Brown, *Working Ethics: Strategies for Decision Making and Organizational Responsibility,* San Francisco: Jossey-Bass Publishers, 1990.

[23] Brown, p. 32.

[24] Brown, p. 34.

[25] Brown, p. 37.

[26] Brown, p. 37.

[27] Brown, pp. 47-49.

[28] Brown, p. 197.

[29] Brown, pp. 180-204.

[30] See Juergensmeyer, pp. 163-166, for a helpful introduction to mediation literature.

[31] Readers might wonder how these comments on the open-ended curiosity of civil process square with my comments on fallibilism in chapter six. There, remember, I said that fallibilism was part of the enlightenment argument for civility. I suggested that a religious believer did not have to accept fallibilism in order to care deeply for the political opponent; the religious believer only had to accept as truth some doctrine (such as Christian dogma) that required one to care for the political opponent. But now it seems that I am endorsing fallibilism by another name, i.e. openness to learning. I do think we should be fallibilists, but I also think civility can be maintained without fallibilism.

My position is not really self-contradictory. Civility, a virtue that prizes the good of the political opponent, can indeed be grounded in a firmly held, non-fallibilistic, comprehensive doctrine. Whether a particular non-fallibilist does care for the political opponent will depend on the actual nature of the comprehensive doctrine the believer embraces. Some conceptions of the good support civility, and some do not.

Civil process, on the other hand, does require openness to learning, i.e. fallibilism. The burden of this chapter has been to show how civil process supports civility. So: while civility may be grounded in a non-fallibilist conception of the good, it is better grounded in a fallibilist worldview, since fallibilists will be ready to participate in civil process.

Chapter Eight:

Civility and Coercion

> Christian civility takes human freedom seriously. I may want people to believe as I do about some basic matters—but what I want is for them to *choose* to see things that way. This means that I must rely on testimony and persuasion in presenting my views to them. Civil Christians will be very reluctant to endorse moral and religious programs that rely on coercion. —Richard Mouw[1]

In this passage, Richard Mouw writes to evangelical Christians, not professional philosophers or a general public. But his words ought to be considered by wider audiences; they express well the temper of civility toward a crucial question. The question is about coercion, and the right temper is reluctance—and it is the purpose of this chapter to discuss both.

To situate this discussion, let us recall the definitions of important terms from earlier chapters. We said that "politics" is the art or science of making group decisions; by this broad definition, politics includes office politics, church politics, family politics, state politics, etc. A "political opponent" (I may just say "opponent" or even "enemy") is simply someone who disagrees with someone else in some political decision-making process. "Civility" is a political virtue, a character trait that moves one to treat her political opponents well.

Suppose we desire to develop within ourselves this virtue of civility. How ought we, as people who nurture within us a desire to treat our opponents well, think about coercion? Human beings almost universally dislike being coerced, so it is easy to see that coercion of others will be problematic for anyone who is genuinely civil. If I want to treat others well, I will want to treat them as I desire to be treated (the golden rule), so I will be reluctant to coerce them. Some, such as Mohandas Gandhi, would go further and say that civil people would never coerce others. But that goes too far. To see why, we should examine coercion more carefully.

Some Varieties of Coercion

Here is another definition. Coercion, let us say, is causing someone to act or believe against his will.

Philosophy of mind suggests that this definition is beset with many difficulties. What is freedom of will? What does it mean to act or believe in accord with one's will? What does it mean to *not* act or believe in accord with one's will? How do other persons cause such things? And so on. I am not going to address any of these questions. I assume that there is such a thing as free will. I assume that we can, in a rough and ready way at least, distinguish between actions and beliefs a person freely chooses and actions and beliefs which others compel her to take.[2]

A central question of political philosophy is this: under what conditions is it right for a government to coerce its own citizens or the citizens of another country? History is replete with instances of tyranny and oppression, so philosophers want to work out a theory that distinguishes between unjust and just coercion. But remember the broad notion of "politics" with which I am working. The virtue of civility applies not just to state politics, but also to the politics of the corporation and the non-profit research group—any group of people that needs to make a decision. Accordingly, before examining possible justifications of coercion, I want to assemble some reminders of the many ways people coerce each other. Consider this list.

1. In business politics: contracts. Valid contracts are entered into freely, so one might object that contracts do not cause people to act

against their will. But if parties fail to see all the possible consequences of the contract promises they make, they may over time come to feel the contract compelling them to do other than what they want. Usually, we think it is entirely just to require parties to fulfill their contracts, even if they find them burdensome, but we should nevertheless observe that contracts coerce. We should also be aware that the underlying notion of a contract has been a prime ingredient in philosophical justifications of state coercion.

2. In family politics: the will. In her long life, Grandma has accumulated an estate. She decides which relatives, friends or charitable organizations will receive various items from her estate. Her decisions are binding on the recipients. One person does not get what he wanted, and another gets what she did not want. Notice that the coercive nature of a will depends much less on mutual consent than a contract.

3. In electoral politics: the vote. (Think here, not just of electoral state politics, but also of elections in organizations like corporations, both for-profit and non-profit.) Candidate Smith wants some office, and Jones' vote for some other candidate may prevent Smith from gaining the office, thus causing her to do what she does not will, or, which amounts to the same thing, preventing her from doing what she wills. We ought to note that coercive acts vary in at least two ways. First, if Jones persuades others to vote against Smith, his actions are more coercive than if he had only voted against her himself, in the sense that his actions are more likely to deprive her of what she wills. We might label this feature the "strength" of the coercion; some coercive acts are stronger than others. Second, Jones' actions can be more coercive if they deprive Smith of more things or more important things than just a political office. He could, for example, in the process of campaigning against Smith, slander her or threaten her children. We can call this the "severity" of the coercion.

Notice an important difference between the strength of a coercion and its severity. The more severe a coercion is, the harder it is to justify. Consider the example just given. As a coercive action, Jones' vote against Smith is easy to justify, since Smith consented to the process of an election when she entered the race. But Jones' threats against Smith's children are harder, perhaps impossible, to justify, because they deprive her of a more fundamental desire (that her children be safe). In contrast to the severity of a coercion, the strength of a coercion does not matter when it comes to justification. If it is just to attempt to compel a person against her will at all, it is just to do so effectively. It often happens that a more severe coercion is also a stronger (more effective) coercion, and such actions require greater justification, but only because they are more severe, not because they are stronger.

We need to remember this bit about the severity of coercion. The more severe a coercion is, the better its justification needs to be.

4. In community politics: the civil suit. Legal judgments obviously coerce, but the adversarial nature of a suit—plaintiff vs. defendant—may obscure the political nature of the court of law. When a judge appeals to the common law or to a statute to decide a dispute in the community, the decision sets or reaffirms a precedent that applies not just to the parties in the dispute, but also to future parties in similar situations. By building up a settled body of common law, a society decides its course; that is, it makes political decisions.

5. In international politics: boycotts, embargoes, economic sanctions, and military force. No one would dispute that these are coercive actions, and some are stronger and/or more severe than others.

6. In family politics: involuntary commitment. This coercive act also plays a role in the politics of institutions like mental hospitals. The state, through the court system, may also be involved. We are reminded that the institutions of society often interweave with each other; sometimes there is no clear line between the politics of family, hospital and state.

7. In state politics: taxation. Political philosophers write much about distributive justice, and I have no desire to add to that literature. It should be clear to all that taxation is coercive (but it isn't clear; see the section on coercion and violence below); people don't want to pay taxes, and they must. We should ask whether and how the justifications which philosophers have offered for this or that conception of distributive justice help us to understand how other kinds of coercion might be justified.

8. In church politics: the congregational vote, the papal decision, the sense of the meeting, etc. Religious polities differ tremendously. In societies that protect freedom of religion, the coercive force of religious decisions depends on individuals' free commitment to the religious body. As with business contracts, we who stand on the outside may think it proper for a religious group to specify its demands for those who choose to affiliate with it. Still, we should see that after a long affiliation the decision of a religious group might act coercively on the faithful.

Without extending it further, I intend this list to hint at the great variety of ways people coerce each other. Life in community requires that we accommodate each other in many ways. Clear mindedness requires that we recognize that some accommodation will not be voluntary; the political community—family, business, church, school, state—will have to coerce recalcitrant individuals. When we ask how coercion might be justified, or what attitude a civil person should take to coercion, we should be mindful of the varieties of coercion.

Coercion and Violence

Several people, when responding to the ideas in this chapter, have objected to one or more of the examples of coercion just listed. For example, several objectors say voting is not coercive. These objectors agree that voting against a candidate is an act intended to keep the candidate from holding some office, but that isn't coercion, they say. Real coercion contains a threat of violent force that seems absent in voting. Candidates for office willingly submit themselves to a majority decision when they choose to run for office, so they don't need to be compelled to accept the voters' rejection.

In a similar way, other respondents have objected to listing business contracts as coercive. The parties to a contract enter it voluntarily, so only if some party to a contract reneges on his promise does he need to be compelled to fulfill the contract.

Again, others might object to listing tax collection as coercive. As Oliver Wendell Holmes said, taxes are the price we pay to live in civilized society—that is, we implicitly agree to them when we accept the goods of a commonwealth.

These objections share common threads of thought about coercion, violence and justification. Perhaps not every objector shares all these threads, but the threads seem to weave together to create a curtain separating voting or contracts or taxes from coercion. First, they assume that coercion involves a threat of violent compulsion. Second, they assume that violence is *prima facie* wrong, so that it must be justified to be morally acceptable. (Perhaps there are many ways in which violence could be justified, or maybe only a few, or just one. However justification happens, the point is that violence needs justification.) So, third, coercion is morally problematic; since it threatens violence, it always stands in need of justification. But, say the objectors, voting, contracts, and taxation don't seem morally problematic. There's no threat of violence, and no particular need for justification.

I say these ideas *seem* to weave together—but in fact they are confused. The second assumption is all right; violence is *prima facie* wrong and requires justification. But the first assumption, that coercion relies on a threat of violence, is unclear. Is it only explicit threats of violence that are wrong? At least some implied threats of violence are also *prima facie* wrong, requiring justification. And there are implied threats even in voting. Suppose that the loser of a presidential election in some country refused to accept the outcome of that election. We can well imagine (since this has actually happened many times) that the winning candidate, once in office, might violently compel the loser to accept the election results. So how is it that voting is not coercive?

The objectors err first when they attribute the wrongness of coercion to violence or threats of violence. Coercion is *prima facie* wrong just because it overrides a person's free choice; the additional wrong of violence may or may not be present.

The objectors also err because they overlook the justifications of some coercions, probably because those justifications are so overwhelming and obvious. Voting is easily justified, precisely because candidates have voluntarily submitted themselves to a democratic procedure. When the justification is so obvious, we are tempted to overlook it. We shouldn't. When we vote, we attempt to compel persons against their will, and this coercion would be wrong if there were no justification for it.

All coercion needs moral justification, and the more severe it is, the more stringent is the requirement of justification.

How Should Coercion Be Justified?

Nancey Murphy and George Ellis, in their book, *On the Moral Nature of the Universe*, present what they call a kenotic view of God.[3] To preserve human freedom, they say, God empties himself of divine power in his dealings with the universe. God is a persuading God, not a compelling God. Since Christian ethics takes its basic values from God's nature, pacifism looms large in the view of ethics which Murphy and Ellis offer as a unifying structure between the natural and social sciences.

I start my discussion of the justification of coercion with Murphy and Ellis's non-coercive God for two reasons. First, their ethic comes close to saying that human beings ought never to coerce each other. I don't think they want to go that far, but if they did, they would illustrate one endpoint in the debate spectrum, the position that coercion can never be justified. The other end of the spectrum would be Callicles' position in *Gorgias*, that any effective coercion is just coercion: might makes right. Second, Murphy and Ellis unabashedly offer a philosophically sophisticated religious ethic. Pacifism is right for human beings, they say, because of certain truths about God. If it is true that people ought not to coerce each other or that they ought to be reluctant to coerce each other, it is because God is non-coercive.

I could have used a different example. Gandhi, if I understand him rightly, *did* think that coercion was never right.[4] Like Murphy and Ellis, Gandhi grounded his political ethics in his religious beliefs.

Murphy and Ellis do not address political philosophy in detail. If they did, we might find them to be non-liberals. They derive their conception of the right from their conception of the good. God, the good, has nature X, so the right thing for humans is to act in accord with X. If applied to politics and coercion, this would mean that any coercion we use ought to accord with the nature of God. Liberal political philosophers find this position intolerable. Murphy and Ellis's God may be non-coercive and kind, but someone else's god may be manipulative and arbitrary. More importantly, liberals say, irresolvable conflicts exist between various conceptions of the good. If we seek to build our political philosophy on the nature of God, or some other kind of ultimate good, given the conflicting conceptions of the ultimate good that people have, our attempts to build political structures will be conflict-ridden and prone to tyranny. To avoid this, liberals traditionally make a priority of right over good (in political philosophy). The liberal state should not try to arbitrate between the various conceptions of the good that citizens hold; rather, it should seek to treat all citizens rightly, that is, by means of a minimal set of procedures that all rational beings can agree to. For instance, the liberal state does not have to decide whose conception of the good is true—in fact, it must separate itself completely from such questions—while it provides fair procedural guidelines for dealings between adherents of differing goods. Of course, in order to make its procedures effective, the state has to coerce citizens. So, while the liberal state will not justify coercion on the basis of some notion of the good, it still needs some justification of coercion.

Since Hobbes, many liberals have tried to justify state coercion by appeal to some form of consent. In business, remember, we think it just to force someone to fulfill the terms of a contract if he freely consented to it. Social contract theory builds on this intuition. It is right to compel people, says social contract theory, not only on the basis of some particular contract between historical parties, but on the basis of a general contract holding between all members of a society.

The social contract is not historical, philosophers say, but a rational idealization of how political structures are to be justified. As an idealization, the social contract not only explains why it is just for the state to coerce its citizens, it also gives grounds for the criticism and improvement of social institutions and procedures. For example, we might suppose that an accurate poll of some oppressed group—the African Americans of Alabama in 1910, or the women of Saudi Arabia of 1990—might show a majority of that group approving of the very rules and institutions which restrict them. The social contract philosopher does not think this actual consent (supposing it could be empirically shown) justifies the rules or institutions in question. We have to ask what rules and institutions would be accepted by well-informed and rational persons. (Oppressed groups, we assume, are not well informed.) Of course, philosophers have offered many versions of the social contract, the most famous recent one being John Rawls' "original position." The crucial move in all these idealizations is to ask what social rules or virtues people would approve given certain conditions.

Let us call all such social contracts "ideal consents." Obviously, each one depends, for its intended use (in justifying coercion and supplying grounds for social critique) and for its persuasiveness, on its particular notion of what a well-informed and rational person would be like. When it comes to coercion, an ideal consent position says, in effect, that all rational people would approve of the coercion in question, if they were only rational enough and well enough informed. This is explicit, for instance, in Rousseau's notion of the "general will." A person being coerced (say, a thief being sentenced in court) may not actually understand the justice of the coercion, but he could—on the condition that he were more rational or well informed. This is why Robert Audi, when he proffers his "rule of secular rationale," says that religious persons ought not to give religious reasons when they argue for freedom-limiting laws.[5]   A person finding his freedom restricted by a law based on religious reasons would never be able to understand the justice of that law, no matter how rational or well-informed he might be; rather, he would have to be converted. The ideal consent position, which has dominated the liberal political tradition, holds that the justificatory reasoning behind freedom-restricting laws ought to be open to everyone, without requiring conversion to some other worldview—again, on the condition that he is sufficiently rational and well informed.

I think we ought to be philosophically suspicious of ideal consents. I have been convinced, by Alasdair MacIntyre and others, that when Enlightenment philosophers talk about being more rational they promulgate particular notions of practical reason, not the dictates of reason itself. Autonomous reason, "reason itself," is a myth. Pay close attention when a philosopher specifies the conditions for some version of ideal consent. Those conditions will reflect either 1) the narrow, bloodless constraints of basic logic—which will never justify coercion, or 2) a more full-bodied conception of the good—which may well justify coercion, but which violates the liberal conceit of right over good.

There are a number of philosophers—Habermas, Ackerman, Kingwell, etc.[6] —who are trying to remedy this situation by devising some description of the conditions for dialogue between different groups in a pluralistic society. These conditions must not depend on any particular substantive conception of the good, and yet they must be strong enough to justify coercion, at least to the extent that political dialogue is protected against deceit and manipulation. We can expect such philosophers to continue this effort for some time, but if MacIntyre is right—that the enlightenment project cannot succeed—their quest will fail.

Suppose we abandon this quest. If we give up the search for ideal consent, that is, the search for the conditions of consent that do not depend on any substantive conception of the good, are we then required to join Murphy and Ellis in their non-liberalism (on the assumption, as noted above, that Murphy and Ellis are non-liberals)? Does the liberal political tradition stand or fall with ideal consent when it comes to justifying coercion? Not necessarily. Liberalism's heart is its commitment to political liberty and equality, not the social contract justification of these values. Abandoning the quest for ideal consent means that liberals need to find some other ground for their commitment to political liberty and equality.

All serious conceptions of justice will depend on some substantive notion of the good. Liberals deceive themselves if they think a society can establish justice while maintaining neutrality toward the various conceptions of the good. Justice often requires coercion, and sometimes we coerce other people because of the particular notion of the good that we hold; we should not deceive ourselves into thinking otherwise. Instead of enshrining the priority of right over good, liberals should simply admit that any conception of the good that can support certain values, such as commonwealth, civility, autonomy and democracy, can contribute to liberal society.

I suggest that liberals look to real, historical consents rather than ideal consents as justifications of coercion. Liberals should hold, I suggest, two beliefs. First, coercion is sometimes justified by actual consent. Second, actual consents can be better or worse; better consents provide better justification for coercion.

In business, people can consent to a contract expressly, by signature on paper or by word. They also can enter a contract by their actions, and sometimes merely refraining from an action over a period of time is consent to a contract. By analogy, then, we might say that people enter social contracts in a variety of ways. An immigrant who takes a citizenship oath and an employee who signs an employment contract enter those potentially coercive relationships expressly. An immigrant who does not apply for citizenship still consents to the coercive laws of her new country by moving there. And so on.

The idea of implied consent is as old as Plato's *Crito*. But remember that we are thinking about real consents, not ideal ones. It is possible for consent to be implied, not explicit, and yet real and the ground for a just coercion. For instance, if I own a field and the neighbor's cattle routinely trespass across the corner of my lot on their way to water and I do nothing to prevent this trespass, after some time it is possible that I will have granted an implied easement across my property. I may be required by a court to pay for that easement when I put up a fence that keeps the neighbor's cattle from the water. However, the fact that implied consent can be real does not make the implied consent an ideal consent, nor does it transform some philosopher's notion of ideal consent into a real consent. Some philosophers write as if confused on this point. First, they describe some notion of ideal consent. Then they note, as I have, that some consents are implied. Then they conclude that the ideal consent is real, having been implied by some act common to most people (e.g. living in a state without trying to emigrate). Such arguments are obviously fallacious.

The common law says implied consents can be real consents, producing real contracts, but the action (or non-action) that creates the consent must be reasonably related to the contract. The law's "reasonable person" test asks whether a reasonable person would understand the action or non-action to imply a real consent. There is a big difference between the property owner's implied consent to the easement for his neighbor's cattle and the supposed implied consent of a peasant who doesn't try to emigrate from some country.

(An aside. One might ask whether the common law's use of the reasonable person test isn't as philosophically suspicious as any enlightenment philosopher's appeal to autonomous reason. It might be, and often is. That is, legal philosophers have often conceived the reasonable person as an embodiment of autonomous reason without recognizing that they were merely reifying the standards and values of their particular tradition of practical reason. But the common law needn't be so philosophically confused. A "reasonable person" may be admitted to be reasonable according to this or that tradition of rationality. Recent court decisions have moved in this direction by applying a "reasonable woman" test in some cases.)

Real consents—implied or express—vary greatly. We should think of a wide spectrum of consents, ranging from situations of well informed, conscious, deliberate contracts to situations that involve no or almost no consent at all. We don't have to sort them out in detail to say there are differences among consents and that some consents are better than others. And when coercion is under consideration, better consents supply better justifications for coercion.

What are the good-making features of consent that make some consents better than others? This question can only be answered from within some tradition of practical reason or another, though we may hope there will be overlap between traditions. As a Christian in the early 21st century who has been influenced by the western liberal tradition, it seems to me that better consents are those which are express, well-informed, not made under threat, and unhurried, rather than those which are implied, based on misinformation, made under threat, or rushed. There may be other markers of good consents; I'm not giving a complete list. Few consents have all the good-making features, and few have none; again, we are to imagine a wide spectrum of consents, from very good to very bad or even non-existent.

Liberals should hold, I reiterate, that some coercion is justified by real consent, and better consents provide better justification for coercion. So Jones' coercive action of voting against Smith is justified by Smith's consent, which she gave, at least implicitly, when she entered the race for office. Jones's coercive action of slandering Smith is not justified by her consent. People who own property in a country may be thought to consent to the coercive power of that country, a consent that may justify taxation and various regulations on the use of property. (This is not to say that all taxes or regulations *are* just, only that if they are just their justification may rest on real consent.) The coercions of a religious group have better justification in a society with religious freedom, because there a person's consent to that religion is better, than in a society where adherence to religion is unfree.

Liberals should recognize, though, that real consent will not justify some coercion. For example, when a family commits some family member to an institution against that person's will, the coercion may be based on no real consent, express or implied. Rather, the family holds some conception of the good that specifies certain notions of physical and mental health. The involuntary commitment is just only if the idea of mental health motivating the coercion is true—or at least much closer to truth than the patient's idea of proper mental functioning. After therapy, the patient may come to approve of the involuntary commitment, but retroactive consent is as unreal as ideal consent. Putting someone in hospital now is not just because she may come to approve later; that would make all effectively manipulative therapies just therapies.

Consider the application of coercive law to a peasant in medieval Europe, ancient Egypt, or Shogun-era Japan. Governments and upper classes in those times coerced peasants, sometimes in the most severe ways. But such coercion cannot be justified by consent, since the peasant had no way to consent. To the peasant, the existence of the government, the truth about the gods, the necessity of daily labor, indeed, the whole way of the world was a given. To speak of such people consenting to the social contract makes as much sense as saying they consented to air. Now, we may think that along with all the unjust coercion in ancient Egypt (to take one particular) there also may have been some just coercion of unconsenting peasants. But we cannot justify that coercion by appeal to real consent, or by appeal to ideal consent. Liberals should recognize the limits of social contract theorizing. If there was just coercion in ancient Egypt, it was just because of its grounding in some true good.

Again, most international coercion like embargoes or boycotts cannot be justified on the basis of real consent. The world is changing in this regard, and we may hope for a day in which the application of coercive international law rests on widespread consent to international authority. But we should recognize that much actual international coercion has no basis in real consent. And we should resist the conceit that it can be justified by appeal to some ideal consent. International coercion is based on notions of the good, and it is just only if those notions are to some degree true.

To briefly recapitulate: some coercion can be justified by appeal to real consent, and some real consents are better than others, thus giving better justification for coercion. But some coercion is only justified by the good, as it is understood by those coercing. We should be suspicious of ideal consents, as they mask covert appeals to some notion of the good.

Civility and Coercion

A virtue is not a rule, so we should not think that we will be able to capture the relationship between civility and coercion by some rule or decision procedure. Virtues are character traits, and we better understand them as we see their connections with emotions, beliefs, and intentions. A fully satisfying analysis of civility and coercion, then, would take more space than we have here. Nevertheless, I will suggest three tendencies—rather than rules—that describe a civil person's attitude toward coercion. These tendencies express the basic temper of civility toward coercion, which is "reluctance"—Richard Mouw's word.

First, a civil person will favor persuasion over coercion. Mouw is right. If we take freedom seriously, no matter how much we want our political opponent to come to see things as we see them, we will want the opponent's genuine, unforced agreement. This means a civil person will not only favor persuasion over coercion, she will seek to treat her opponent well even as she tries to persuade. She will avoid deception and manipulation.

But we must go further. Like Gandhi, a civil person will not see her conflict with her opponent primarily in terms of winning or losing, but as an opportunity to pursue truth.[7] Her policy will be one of inclusion, inviting the opponent to join in the search for truth-based solutions. The goal of politics, since it is the art of making group decisions, is better decisions, not imposing one's will or gaining power for one's party. The civil person admits that the political opponent brings a perspective to the debate that she doesn't have. The opponent knows things she doesn't know. The civil person has discovered that the political opponent is thus a resource or a partner for better decision-making.

Notice here a connection between the virtue, civility, and a certain belief. I said that the goal of politics is better decisions rather than winning or gaining power. It might be better to say that civil people typically believe this. They believe it is better to lose, if that's what it takes to make better decisions, than to win, if winning is only enforcing their policy or program. Like Socrates, they believe that moral truth is real and worthy of pursuit, even if, like Gandhi, they are always ready to revise their understanding of what the truth is.[8]

Second, if persuasion fails, a civil person will favor coercion that can be justified by better (real) consent over coercion that can only be justified by poor consent or no consent at all.

Gandhi, and perhaps others, would stop at persuasion. All coercion, even the desire to coerce, is *himsa*, he thought.[9] Possibly I will only reveal misunderstanding of Gandhi's ideas here, but it seems to me that he neglected to notice the great variety and reach of coercion in human life. It seems that *ahimsa*, Gandhi's ideal, would not only preclude one from violence or hatred, but also from voting, writing a will, committing a family member to a hospital, and other things we ordinarily consider just. Certainly, Gandhi's political opponents thought some of his tactics were coercive, such as mass marches, boycotts, and strikes. So I don't think that *ahimsa* describes the civil person's approach to the political enemy. Sometimes we may justifiably coerce the opponent. When we do, the justification will usually come from some real consent, and civil people will want better consents.

Third, a civil person will recognize that some coercion cannot be justified by any real consent. In such cases, her reluctance to coerce will be greater than ever. She may regard some classes of coercive actions as simply unjustifiable without real consents. Such coercions are judged as too severe, in the sense described above, to be justifiable. In such cases, the civil person would adopt a rule against such actions. For instance, a civil person might reject the death penalty; her civility would be partially expressed in efforts to abolish capital punishment. Other civil people might consider the questionable coercive actions as possibly justifiable, but they would agree that the more severe a coercion is, the greater should be our reluctance to use it.

Note that in speaking of "justification" for coercive actions that cannot be justified by any real consent, we have left behind the social contract tradition and any notion of right over good. If such actions are justifiable, it is because they conform, at least to some degree, to the good. Civil people ought to recognize that their political opponents may not share the conception of the good under which they contemplate coercion. Civil people ought to remember that the political opponent, the target of the contemplated coercion, can be a partner and resource in the search for truth. So it is with fear and trembling that a civil person will venture to compel the political opponent against the opponent's will in the absence of real consent. Nevertheless, it is possible that such coercion is justifiable; indeed, one may have a moral duty to so coerce the opponent.

Addendum: Civility and Pacifism

I have just said that civil people may sometimes have moral duties to coerce their opponents. This raises questions about the most severe form of coercion, war.

What is the relationship between civility and war? Must a civil person, one who desires to treat her political opponents well, be a pacifist? Or is it enough to revert to Mouw's word again and say that civil people are *reluctant* to fight wars?

Let us define pacifism as the moral rejection of all wars, and let us use "war" in its usual sense of conflicts between nations or large groups that produce many violent deaths and injuries. This definition of pacifism is silent about many topics which are often linked to discussions of war: capital punishment, violence, or self-defense. There are varieties of pacifists; some reject killing, some reject police force, others reject violence, still others reject all coercion, but all unite in rejecting war. A pacifist, then, is a person who has adopted a certain moral rule, a rule that condemns all wars.

As I said above, a virtue is not a rule. So if pacifism consists in a moral rule ("no wars"), the virtue of civility cannot be equated with pacifism. Pacifism is not sufficient for civility; adopting such a rule will not make someone civil. Nor is it necessary; persons may pursue civility, even incorporate this virtue into their character, while still believing that some wars are morally permissible. But what I have said in this chapter about civility and coercion helps show why the pursuit of civility may lead people to adopt the pacifist's rule.

War is the most severe form of coercion we know. War coerces by depriving the enemy of many goods, goods of the most important kinds. War creates orphans, spreads disease, destroys public and private property (art works, museums, farms, books, etc.), and encourages hatred and desire for revenge. As the most severe form of coercion, war requires more justification than any other coercion.

It's clear that war cannot be justified by any appeal to consent. The persons who most suffer the outrages of war—soldiers, urban workers, peasant farmers, and children—are almost never the persons who decide to initiate war. We might deem the decision makers who start a war to have consented to the violence of the enemy, but it is hard to see how their real consent (let us not impute to them any ideal consent) to violence justifies the suffering of ordinary women, men, and children.

War as coercion, if justifiable at all, must be justified by appeal to some conception of the good. Only if that conception of the good is true, or much more nearly true than the ideology of the enemy, could war be just. Often, almost always in fact, people have defended their war making in just such terms: they fight for the good, while their enemies are the incarnation of evil. But these are rhetorical flourishes attendant to war making; it's hard to take them seriously as moral philosophy. How could the morally serious warrior *know* that her conception of the good was true enough to justify the extreme coercions of war?

In chapter one, remember, I asked the same question about the American Civil War. I suggested that the abolitionist (against slavery, abortion, nuclear weapons, capital punishment, or whatever) could gain moral knowledge through a process of dialogue with the political opponent. The political opponent is a resource, an aid; his challenges to one's beliefs test those beliefs and make them candidates for moral knowledge. But warfare, by its nature, renders political dialogue almost impossible. It seems that a civil person will harbor great doubts that the good for which he fights really justifies the extreme coercions of war. He may conscientiously conclude that the only safe route is to rule out war making entirely.

Other civil persons may conclude that in some rare cases the evil of the enemy is so clear that war, in spite of its horrors, must be used to stop them. To them, Mouw's word will apply. They will be reluctant to approve of wars, remembering how often human beings have convinced themselves that their cause was just while they were fighting, and how seldom it was judged to be so afterward.

Notes

[1] Mouw, Richard, Uncommon *Decency: Christian Civility in an Uncivil World*, Downers Grove, Illinois: Intervarsity Press, 1992, p. 143.

[2] For a survey and critique of various positions related to freedom of the will, readers may consult Laura Waddell Ekstrom, *Free Will: A Philosophical Study*. Boulder, Colorado: Westview Press, 2000.

[3] George F. R. Ellis and Nancey Murphy, *On the Moral Nature of the Universe*, Minneapolis, MN: Fortress Press, 1996.

[4] Juergensmeyer, Mark, *Fighting Fair: A Non-Violent Strategy for Resolving Everyday Conflicts*. Previously published as *Fighting with Gandhi*, San Francisco: Harper and Row, 1986, pp. 28-29.

[5] Robert Audi, "The Place of Religious Argument in a Free and Democratic Society," *San Diego Law*, Vol. 30, No. 4, Fall, 1993, pp. 691-692. See the discussion of Audi's rules in chapter four.

[6] See chapter five.

[7] Juergensmeyer, pp. 18-26.

[8] See *Phaedo* 90de, for Socrates' attitude, and Juergensmeyer, p. 26, for Gandhi's.

[9] Juergensmeyer, p. 27.

Chapter Nine:

What Next?

To some readers, this book probably feels thin. Such readers look for precise, compelling arguments when they read philosophy, and such arguments may seem lacking here. Only when criticizing Mark Kingwell's reading of MacIntyre (in chapter five) do I come close to the kind of technical precision some people take to be the hallmark of good philosophical work. Instead, the movement of this book depends on stipulative definitions: of civility, of politics, of political opponent, of the telos of politics, and of coercion. This is not an accident, but a deliberate outworking of some beliefs I have about philosophical method.

It seems to me that many philosophers, past and present, labor to produce what might be called "knock down" arguments. That is, they aim to find arguments that would be compelling to any rational person, provided that the reader made the effort to understand the arguments. Like Descartes, they hope that if philosophers could just hit on the right method in philosophy, truth would have to emerge. Often, it seems, they think that right method involves greater and greater measures of logical acuity and linguistic precision. I have nothing against cogency or clarity, but I think we ought to recognize the limits of argument.

I think the ambition of finding the perfect rational method, and universally compelling arguments based on it, is unrealistic. Many thinkers have pointed out the utopian quality of the philosophical dream of rationally compelling method. As I pointed out in chapter six, this is a commonplace notion in "postmodernism." We are getting used to the idea that what counts as good reasoning or good evidence differs from one tradition of rationality to another. It's not impossible to persuade people using evidence and good reasons, but the people persuaded must accept the standards of evidence and reason used by the arguer. Especially in matters of practical reason—ethics, social theory, politics, etc.—we should expect that the prephilosophical commitments that people bring to the discussion will condition and limit the force of argument.

It is important to emphasize that this perspectivist approach to argument is not epistemic relativism. We can and do persuade each other—rationally persuade each other—but we do so from within our own perspective. The force or attractiveness of one person's argument will depend partially on factors in the other person's mental world, factors beyond the control of the arguer.[1] A rationally persuasive argument must connect with norms of evidence and inference already accessible to the other person, and it must be expressed in terms she understands. Sometimes, then, before giving a compelling argument for a position, we must "come to terms" with our audience. We must explain our ideas in such a way that our readers and listeners can grasp them.

In coming to terms with an audience, it often happens that we need to explain not just one, but many interrelated ideas. For example, consider explaining baseball to someone who has never seen it before.

Many of the important concepts in baseball—base, pitch, hit, fair, foul, run, strike, steal, out, etc.—are to a large extent defined in terms of one another. Sometimes a cluster of concepts is so self-referentially defined that explaining them to someone not already involved in the practice around which the concepts gather gets nowhere. The beginner is urged to try out the activity; by trial and error, with good coaching and further explanations, the beginner picks up the language of the game.[2]

Now, I don't think the cluster of concepts in this book is all that difficult. But they are interwoven, and the plausibility of some depend on their connections with the others. So my task has been not so much to argue for the truth of my position, but to explain it, to show how several interrelated ideas fit together. The book can be read as an extended invitation to the reader to work her way into an interconnected set of concepts. If she does, she may find that as a whole they become plausible.

We may call the concept cluster of this book, naturally enough, the "civility cluster":

1. Civility is a virtue. I endorse the idea that much of the moral life is best explained by reference to virtues. A good life will require many virtues, and among them civility is important.

2. Virtues are functional and teleological. A virtue counts as a virtue because having it tends to help human beings achieve the goods of their practices. Practices aim at ends; hence, teleology.

3. Civility functions in politics. The virtue of civility helps people succeed in politics, and politics, I said, is the business of making group decisions.

4. Politics can be a process that produces truth and peace (i.e. shalom). The telos of politics is not winning, but making better decisions for the group.

5. Civility functions to produce truth and peace in politics. Civility helps political processes by protecting a crucial resource for better political decisions, the opponent.

6. Civility focuses on the political opponent. We are tempted to ignore the stranger, but we are tempted to destroy the opponent. So we greatly need to develop the virtue that moves us to protect the opponent.

7. Civility cannot be reduced to rules about political rationales. Audi's appeal to secular rationales and Kingwell's allegiance to the priority of right over good both try to explain civility as constraints on political speech. Though interesting and informative, neither thinker sees civility as focused on the political opponent.

8. Civility needs to be properly grounded. Since civility is a costly virtue, we need strong motivation to develop it within ourselves. I have suggested that Christian dogma provides adequate grounding for civility; it is possible that readers would approve of the rest of the book and still cling to some other ground for civility.

9. Civility enables and is enabled by a civil process. The principles of civil process apply to all sorts of political situations: families, businesses, negotiations, social movements, and state politics. As with other concept clusters, people may come to a better grasp of the concepts of civility as they practice civil processes.

10. Civility produces reluctance to coerce. Some forms of coercion may be completely unacceptable to civil people; in any case, civil people will prefer persuasion to coercion, and they will prefer coercion justified by real consent to coercion justified only by appeal to the good.

What Next?

I have not produced the last word on civility. At most, I hope to have said something that will begin to produce some order among the many voices that talk about civility. If the civility cluster as I have described it is at least plausible, several avenues for further reflection open before us. I invite the reader to explore them.

First, what is the relationship between civility and other virtues? Since civility can be costly, we might expect courage to be necessary for civil people. In chapter seven, I suggested that civility is partner to hope, curiosity, and confidence in the opponent. Hope is often thought of as a virtue; is it necessary for civility? Should we think of curiosity and confidence as virtues? If so, how do we analyze them? How do we develop them?

Second, what is the relationship between civility and emotions? According to the definition I introduced in chapter two, civility is a character trait that moves a person to treat political opponents well or to feel emotions that move a person to treat political opponents well. I said very little about what those constituent emotions might be. Love? Respect? Generosity? Awe? Do some emotions work better than others when it comes to civility? Which emotions tend to retard civility? Fear? Anger? Of course, sorting out which emotions help and which hinder only leads to the practical question of how to engender the better emotions in ourselves.

Third, how does civility relate to beliefs? I said in chapter seven that civil people typically believe that the opponent can be a resource for better decision making. Uncivil people, I suppose, may believe the opposite: that they are able to propose good policies for the group without the input of their political opponents. What other beliefs are typical of civil people? Suppose it turns out that some belief, let's call it belief B, is often or always held by civil people, and suppose further that some person does not hold belief B. Can that person develop civility anyway? There are all kinds of complications to consider here.

Fourth, and most important, how do we practice civility? At many points in the book, I have suggested situations in which we might practice civility: in business, negotiations, families, etc. But what does that really mean, to practice civility? How does one go about training oneself to feel appropriate emotions? Questions of praxis apply to all virtues, as Aristotle noted, for it is by repeating appropriate actions that good deeds become habits of character.

Many people praise civility nowadays, though there seems to be confusion as to what it is. If this little book has given the reader some tools for seeing through that confusion, it will have served a good purpose. If it provokes one or more readers to desire and pursue civility, it will have achieved all I might reasonably hope.

Notes

[1] Note that we often speak of the "force" of an argument. Might we not be better off to speak of the "attractiveness" of an argument? The difference between these two metaphors catches much of the point I am trying to make.

[2] Obviously, by speaking of "game," I allude to Wittgenstein's famous notion of "language games."

Bibliography

"A Tale of Two Martyrs," *Christian History*. Vol. XIV, No. 4: pp. 18-19.

Audi, Robert. "The Place of Religious Argument in a Free and Democratic Society." *San Diego Law Review*. Vol. 30, No. 4 Fall, 1993: 677-702.

Barber, Benjamin. *A Place for Us*. New York: Hill and Wang, 1998.

Brown, Marvin T. *Working Ethics: Strategies for Decision Making and Organizational Responsibility,* San Francisco: Jossey-Bass Publishers, 1990.

Cahoon, Lawrence. "Civic Meetings, Cultural Meanings." *Civility*. Ed. Leroy S. Rouner. Notre Dame, Indiana: University of Notre Dame Press, 2000.

Carter, Stephen L. *Civility: Manners, Morals, and the Etiquette of Democracy*. New York: Basic Books, 1998.

Delattre, Edwin J. "Civility and the Limits to the Tolerable." *Civility*. Ed. Leroy S. Rouner. Notre Dame, Indiana: University of Notre Dame Press, 2000.

Doehring, Carrie. "Civility in the Family." *Civility*. Ed. Leroy S. Rouner. Notre Dame, Indiana: University of Notre Dame Press, 2000.

Dupre´, Louise. *Passage to Modernity*. New Haven, Connecticut: Yale University Press, 1993.

Ekstrom, Laura Waddell. *Free Will: A Philosophical Study*. Boulder, Colorado: Westview Press, 2000.

Ellis, George F. R. and Nancey Murphy. *On the Moral Nature of the Universe*. Minneapolis, MN: Fortress Press, 1996.

Fisher, Roger, William Ury, and Bruce Patton, *Getting to Yes: Negotiating Agreement Without Giving I.,* 2nd. ed. New York: Penguin Books, 1991.

Fox, George. *The Journal of George Fox.* Rev. John L. Nickals. London: London Yearly Meeting, 1975.

Hauerwas, Stanley. *The Peaceable Kingdom.* Notre Dame, Indiana: University of Notre Dame Press, 1983.

Heilbronner, Robert and Lester Thurow, *Economics Explained.* New York: Touchstone Books, 1998.

Juergensmeyer, Mark. *Fighting Fair: A Non-Violent Strategy for Resolving Everyday Conflicts.* New York: Harper and Row, 1986.

Kingwell, Mark. *A Civil Tongue: Justice, Dialogue, and the Politics of Pluralism.* University Park, Pennsylvania: The Pennsylvania State Press, 1995.

Koivisto, Rex. *One Lord, One Faith: A Theology for Cross-Denominational Renewal.* Wheaton, Illinois: Victor Books/SP Publications, Inc. 1993.

Life Magazine, June 1992.

MacIntyre, Alasdair. *After Virtue.* 2nd Ed. Notre Dame, Indiana: University of Notre Dame Press, 1984.

---. *Whose Justice? Which Rationality?* Notre Dame, Indiana: University of Notre Dame Press, 1988.

Marsden, George. *Religion and American Culture.* Fort Worth, Texas: Harcourt Brace College Publishers, 1990.

Martin, Dennis. "Catholic Counterpoint: What was it like to be on the losing side of England's Reformation?" *Christian History.* Vol. XIV, No. 4.

Mouw, Richard. *Uncommon Decency: Christian Civility in an Uncivil World.* Downers Grove, Illinois: Intervarsity Press, 1992.

Murphy, Andrew R. *Conscience and Community: Revisiting Toleration and Dissent in Early Modern England and America.* University Park, Pennsylvania: The Pennsylvania State University Press, 2001.

Plantinga, Alvin. *Warrant: the Current Debate.* New York: Oxford University Press, 1993.

---. *Warrant and Proper Function .* New York: Oxford University Press, 1993.

Quinn, Philip L. "Political Liberalisms and Their Exclusions of the Religious." The Presidential Address delivered at the 93rd Annual Central Division Meeting of the American Philosophical Association. *Proceedings and Addresses of the American Philosophical Association.* Vol. 69, No. 2. 47.

Rawls, John. *A Theory of Justice.* Cambridge, Massachusetts: Harvard University Press, 1971.

Roberts, Arthur. "Good and Evil in a World Threatened by Nuclear Omnicide: A Proposed Epistemological Paradigm." Unpublished paper.

Rorty, Richard. *Contingency, Irony, and Solidarit.y* Cambridge: Cambridge University Press, 1989.

Schmidt, James. "Is Civility a Virtue?" *Civility.* Ed. Leroy S. Rouner. Notre Dame, Indiana: University of Notre Dame Press, 2000.

Vanderbilt, Amy. *New Complete Book of Etiquette: A Guide to Contemporary Living.* New York: Doubleday, 1952.

von Rad, Gerhard. *Old Testament Theology.* Vol. 1. New York: Harper & Row, 1962.

Index

Note: The entries for civility and virtue, which appear throughout the book, is not listed in the Index.